The Joy of Stitching

The Joy of Stitching

38 Quick and Easy Embroidery and Needlework Designs

Nina
Granlund
Sæther

SELLERS
PUBLISHING

Published by Sellers Publishing, Inc.

161 John Roberts Road, South Portland, Maine 04106
Visit our Web site: www.sellerspublishing.com
E-mail: rsp@rsvp.com

First published in 2014 as *Raske Sting* by Nina Granlund Sæther
copyright © 2014 CAPPELEN DAMM AS

English translation © 2016 Sellers Publishing, Inc.
All rights reserved.

ISBN 978-1-4162-4577-3
Library of Congress Control Number: 2015946618

Edited by Robin Haywood
English translation by Margaret Berge Hartge

Cover design by Ashley Halsey
Layouts by Charlotte Cromwell
Photography by Guri Pfeifer
Patterns by Nina Granlund Sæther

The instructions, charts, and material lists were carefully reviewed by the author and the editor; however, accuracy cannot be guaranteed. The author and publisher cannot be held liable for errors. Errata will be published on the Web site www.sellerspublishing.com.

10 9 8 7 6 5 4 3 2 1

Printed and bound in China.

Contents

Introduction: Playing with Needle and Thread 8

Tips and Advice 12

Stitches 16

Felt-covered Box with Embroidery 22

Made with Love 24

Sweet Birdie Makeup Bag 26

Colorful Glove Cuffs 28

A Belt with Glorious Roses 30

Handmade Watchband 32

Singing Birdie Napkins 34

Robot Pincushion 36

Royal Crown Pincushion 38

Blue Bracelet with Squares 40

Roll the Dice 42

Beetles and Dragonflies 44

Happy Birds Linen Pillow 46

All You Need Is Love 48

Table Runner Decorated with Wild Parsley 50

For the Math Lover 52

A Trolley Car... 54

Drawstring Canvas Bag with Beetles and Dragonflies 56

Boogie-Woogie Beetle Purse 58

A Square Linen Tablecloth with Blue Triangles 60

A Dachshund in a Sweater 62

Princess Dress with Wild Strawberries... 64

Three Colorful Bracelets 66

Festive Suspenders... 68

Party Corset with Stylized Roses 70

Crocodile Loves Cupcakes... 72

Ladybug Sneakers... 74

A Caged Bird Sings! 76

Embroidered Zipper Bag 78

Happy Birthday Banner... 80

Happy Birthday Crown 82

Theodore Giraffe 84

Denim Jacket with Embroidered Designs... 86

The Princess and the Pea... 88

Embroidered Bed Linens for Baby 90

Prima Ballerina Linen Bag... 92

Resources 94

Patterns... 97

Playing with Needle and Thread

Many of my friends have been wondering what I have been doing for the last few months. Why in the world would a modern woman, in the 21st century, want to write a book on embroidery? They think embroidery is old fashioned; they say it's a sewing technique that belongs to a bygone era. My answer is, "No, absolutely not." Gone are the days when embroidery was all about floral motifs and dreary text. The designs can be as modern as you like.

The embroidery techniques and stitches I share in this book provide a marvelous opportunity to play freely with needle and thread. When you think about it, embroidery can be compared to playing with colored pens or crayons in a coloring book or on a blank sheet of paper. Knitting and weaving techniques have quite limiting restrictions in relation to what can be expressed in embroidery. If you want the distances between the threads or yarn to be acceptable, you have to work with relatively short repetitions. However, when embroidering, almost anything is possible. You can, of course, use repeats in the patterns, but you can also work completely without restrictions — without thinking about sequencing and the length between stitches. The number of available variations is enormous. You can choose to make the finest lines or points, or you can cover large areas with stitches. The stitches can be placed tightly next to each other or far apart. The materials can be coarse or gossamer fine. The expression can be decorative and meticulous or more spontaneous and unstructured. The embroidery can be of a rigid and tight nature or quite playful and naive. It is possible to spread out the embroidery on a surface or seek greater variations in both height and depth so the result becomes almost three-dimensional.

Throughout the ages, women have sought to embellish their clothing and other textiles. Today, when many textiles are produced inexpensively in the Far East, and most of the products are comparatively similar, a little hand stitching can put a personal touch on a garment that is seldom purchased that way. A few stitches transform a mass-produced garment into something unique.

Embroidery, stitching, needlework, and cross-stitch are all different names for what we in Norway simply call embroidery. Regardless, if we cross-stitch with a black floss, or do stem stitches with red floss, we call it embroidery: stitches sewn to decorate a piece of fabric.

I like to use a variety of techniques. I cross-stitch on stiff open-weave canvasses and backstitch on linen. It is not necessary to go to an embroidery store to find something to embroider on! In this book, you will see that I have decorated T-shirts, accessories, and other ready-made clothing, as well as store-bought table linens

Experiment with purses and bags. All kinds of textiles can be decorated as long as you can sew through the material. When you choose a heavy linen for a project, the result will be very different than if you embroider on fine silk or wool felt.

Traditionally, embroidery is viewed as a lot of work where much of the time is spent counting and sewing before the project is finished. All the projects in this book are embroidered using quickly made stitches. None of the projects take a lot of time. The white blouse with red hearts (see p. 24), for example, was completed in an afternoon and evening.

The more I embroider, the more fun it becomes. New ideas pop up constantly. Look around and grab the opportunities to embellish items in your home using your own personal expression.

Mira Granlund Søther

Tips and Advice

EMBROIDERY THREAD

I most frequently sew with mouline thread. It's a high-quality thread and can tolerate rough treatment; it keeps its beauty and structure even after several washes in hot water. It is fun, though, to experiment with other types of threads. Luckily, there are a number of excellent online stores that can supply you with materials (see Resources, p. 94). For variety, you may want to embroider with knitting yarn; I've used it in a few of the projects in this book.

FREEHAND STITCHING

I am not particularly fond of messing around with a pattern that has to be transferred from paper onto fabric before I can sew (but I do provide instructions for transferring patterns on p. 14). I often draw directly onto the fabric. As an alternate approach, I may make a shape from some stiff cardboard that I can trace around. I usually draw only the main shapes and fill in the rest with a freehand style of embroidery.

My most cherished tool, which I have become completely dependent upon, is an invisible fabric marker; the lines you draw will completely disappear in 48 hours (see Resources, p. 94). If you make a mistake while you are using this marker, it is no big deal. The only disadvantage with this type of marker is that you have to embroider quickly. You cannot put your embroidery project aside for a week or two and expect to continue where you left off: The drawing will be gone. However, you can always redraw your design on the fabric or you can use other types of markers noted in the Resources.

My designs have a very lively expression when I embroider freely rather than when I follow a sketched design. Spontaneous embroidering invites play and creativity in the details. The result is not always perfect, but in today's world when most things are machine made, I think the imperfections of handwork are a plus. It should be apparent that something is handmade and stitched with love and joy.

TRANSFERRING PATTERNS

If you are hesitant to embroider without a pattern, there are many methods to use to transfer a design onto the textile you want to embroider. Following are some suggested methods for transfer — find out which one works best for you.

As I have previously mentioned, I do, mostly, freehand embroidery, but sometimes I work out a pattern that I will then follow when I am sewing. In those instances, I start by drawing on cardboard or heavy stock paper, then I cut the drawn pattern out and trace around it onto my fabric. The stiff paper or cardboard makes it easy to move the pattern around, and it can even be used in a mirrored position. If you do not want to cut out the patterns in this book, just transfer the pattern you want to use by copying it onto another sheet of paper. I recommend gluing the copied pattern on some heavy stock paper or cardboard before cutting it out.

You can also use light to transfer a pattern. Just place the pattern on a light box or tape it to a window and trace. If you do not have a light box, it is easy to make a temporary one by putting a piece of glass over a light source. However, it is just as easy to tape the pattern onto an ordinary window. Of course, there must be daylight to use this method, and you have to draw standing up.

If you are using the light method, place the fabric you are going to embroider over the pattern and trace it onto the fabric with a marker. It is best to tape down your fabric as well, so that it does not shift while you are tracing the pattern. Using the light method makes it easier to trace all the pattern's details.

Quilter's freezer paper can be placed on a pattern and then copied using a black permanent marker, or you can copy the pattern using an ink-jet copier. Iron the freezer paper onto the back side of your fabric, so that it attaches to the fabric and stays in place while you copy the pattern.

When you are finished copying, pull the freezer paper carefully off the fabric. You can reuse the freezer paper several times for other motifs.

A wax-free carbon transfer paper, also known as graphite paper or tracing paper, and a tracing wheel is a well-used transfer method for sewing. You place the transfer paper between the pattern and the fabric and run the tracing wheel over the pattern. Small, colored dots are then transferred on to the fabric. This method is the easiest to use if you are transferring long lines.

If you are going to embroider on dark fabrics, using a method that transfers dots will usually work the best. First, transfer the pattern to a thin sheet of plastic, for example, plastic sheets with adhesive, architect's Mylar sheets, plastic stencil sheets, or plastic pockets that you cut apart. Place the plastic sheet over the pattern and punch holes with a needle through the plastic following the pattern's outlines. The needle should not be too thin. Push the eye of the needle into an eraser or a cork to make it easier to hold. It also helps if the surface under your work is porous.

When you are finished punching holes in the plastic sheet, lightly pin it to your fabric and paint over the sheet using a textile paint. Use a flat brush and a good amount of paint to transfer the pattern. The paint should go through the holes and attach to the fabric, but make sure that it does not

bleed. Check to see if there are paint dots on the fabric. The dots will be permanent because you are using permanent textile paint. However, it is easy to scrape off the dots if you make a mistake.

When you are embroidering, work so the lines or dots of your pattern are covered by your embroidery floss.

WITH OR WITHOUT AN EMBROIDERY HOOP?

I belong to the group of embroiderers who prefer to sew without a hoop. However, if you are planning to use a satin stitch or long and short stitches, the results will be significantly better if you use a hoop. When you use a hoop, the fabric stays stretched the whole time you work, so you avoid getting a twisted or buckled design. Without a hoop, your fabric can easily become deformed and puckered while you embroider, and that is unfortunate when you have spent many hours decorating it. As always, it is good to experiment and find out what works best for you.

Stitches

I love hand embroidery, and if you are a beginner, you've come to the right place. Stitching can seem overwhelming at first, but if you slow down and take some time, you'll soon be creating your own designs.

If you're an experienced stitcher, I hope you'll like the designs in this book, and if you're new to stitching, don't be intimidated if you can't sew all the stitches the first time — it takes practice. Most of the designs in this book use a limited number of stitches. If you can master a few basic stitches, like the ones below and on the next few pages, you can embroider most of the projects. If you don't know how to do the stitches in a project, get a little help to learn them or substitute with stitches that you already know.

Running Stitch

This is one of the basic stitches used to outline shapes, as well as create straight and curved lines. First, insert your needle through the back of your fabric at the starting point. Working from right to left, bring the needle up at #1, on the front of the fabric, and down at #2, up at #3, and down at #4; continue up and under the fabric. Put the needle through and repeat until you reach the end of the stitching area.

Running stitches, and the spaces between them, are typically of equal length, but that is not a hard-and-fast rule. You can create a different look by adjusting the length of the space or the stitch.

Backstitch

The backstitch creates a solid line and is a

good stitch to use for lettering or to outline the design. Working left to right (going "backward!"), insert the needle down into the fabric and come up at #1, then "back" down at #2, up at #3. Poke the needle down into the fabric, over about ¼" (6mm), and back up again.

Stem Stitch

These are small, even stitches that run from the left towards the right. Slant your stitches slightly along the drawn line. Always bring your needle up to the left and a little behind the previous stitch, and go down again in the front, making each stitch an equal length. Like its namesake, it's perfect when creating flower stems.

Working left to right, bring the needle up at #1, through #2, and back up at #3. Your #3 thread will lie over stitches #1 and #2. The subsequent stitches will continue to lie on top of the previous stitch.

Chain Stitch

Bring the needle up at your starting point. Insert the needle again at the starting point and bring the tip up a short distance away from the desired length of the stitch. Place the working thread behind the needle and pull the needle through the loop. Repeat the steps to make additional stitches. End the length by making a small anchoring stitch at the end of the final loop to secure it in place, Make sure to keep the floss under the needle.

Couching

This is a clever stitch for outlining and creating spirals, curves, and decorative borders. The stitch often uses two threads: a thicker base thread and a thinner, often different-colored one called the couching thread. Place the heavier foundation thread (if using) along the drawn line and fasten it to the fabric using small, even stitches. Then use your contrasting color, if desired, and sew small, evenly spaced stitches over the base thread.

Blanket Stitch

This is a basic stitch that can be used for edging blankets, edging bed and table linens, and attaching appliqué. A blanket stitch has a top and a bottom. Bring your needle up at the bottom line and bring it to the top right on the upper line.

Pull the needle through, keeping the thread in your left hand. With the floss under the needle, come up again below this point on the lower line.

Pull the thread through to make a square loop; repeat.

Laced Running Stitch

First, sew even running stitches and then make a decorative border by lacing another thread back and forth through the sewn running stitches. It's preferable to use a blunt tapestry needle for this part of the embroidery, and be careful not to stick the needle into the fabric. You can use the same floss and color as the running stitches, or you may choose another color and/or thread to weave in and out.

Seed Stitch

You can fill in an area using these small straight stitches of equal or different lengths. The stitches are sewn in a random pattern and run in all directions.

To make seed stitches, create areas of short running stitches.

Cross-stitch

Come up at the bottom left of the stitch and go down again at the top right. At this point, you have made a tent stitch or half cross-stitch. If you are making just one cross-stitch, come up on the right at the bottom and go down at the top of the stitch on the left. You've just made an X. If you are sewing several cross-stitches in a row, come up at the bottom left and go down at the top right as many times as needed. Then, going back to form the cross, move from the right to the left and come up at the bottom on the right and down at the top on the left until you have completed all the cross-stitches.

French Knot

French knots are so versatile! Use them to create fun, almost 3-D knots in the center of flowers or anywhere you want some texture. To begin, bring the threaded needle through the back of the fabric and up, hold the needle with your non-needle hand and with the other, grab the floss and pull taut. Wrap the floss two or three times around the needle for a small knot and more for a larger one. Turn the needle downward, as if to insert into the fabric. Bring just the tip of the needle inside the fabric, slide the wound thread down to the fabric, all the while holding the thread taut with your other hand. The knot will lie on top of the fabric while the needle continues down to the back of the fabric — this will happen, because you are holding it there with a finger or thumb. The loops (and the knot) will look better if the threads are pulled tight!

Mille Fleur Stitch

A mille fleur is a circular pattern of blanket stitches. This stitch is sewn as chain stitches, but each loop is fastened at the end with a small stitch. The stitch can be sewn as a single stitch or as a group of four or five stitches next to each other, so they create a flower.

Heart Stitch

Stitch two mille fleur stitches next to each other and let the stitches overlap a little so they form a heart.

Satin Stitch

Satin stitches can be sewn with equally long stitches or with stitches of different lengths. These stitches are usually used to fill in an area.

Satin Stitch for Filling in an Area

When you want to completely fill in an area, use satin stitches closely stitched together. The stitches are placed parallel to each other and are adjusted a little to fit curved shapes or bows. Make sure the edges of the shapes are even and sharp.

Long and Short Stitch

If an area is too large or uneven to use satin stitches to fill it in, the long and short stitches work well. Sew, alternating long and short stitches next to each other, in rows to make the embroidered area you want to cover even.

Overcast Stitch

This stitch is used to keep fabric from fraying; it is often the first step in a project. The overcast stitch can be accomplished by hand-sewn stitching or by using your sewing machine. Using thread that matches your fabric, bring the needle from the back through to the front, just below the edge. Loop over the edge, and again bring the thread through from the back to the front. Be careful not to pull too tight or the fabric will crimp. Continue to the end and tie secure knot on the back.

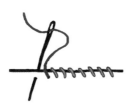

Fly Stitch

This stitch looks like a Y. Come up on the left side at the top of the fabric, hold the floss in place with your left thumb, and bring the needle a little to the right and level with where the thread emerged . Make the stitch on a downward angle so the needle emerges between the two points. Make sure to keep the floss under the needle. Lock the stitch in place by inserting the needle in the middle of the stitch just made.

Closed Blanket Stitch

Sew blanket stitches in groups of two or three so they make triangles.

Trellis with Cross-stitches

Place threads horizontally and vertically, even diagonally, if you choose. Sew a cross-stitch at each point of the intersection. You can use floss of different colors for the trellis and for the crosses.

Projects

Felt-covered Box with Embroidery

A very ordinary cardboard box can be transformed into a beautiful container. With a little wool felt and a few decorative stitches, boring surfaces become textile delights. This pattern can be made to fit larger square boxes if you increase the distance between the lid's outer borders and the circular pattern in the middle.

Materials

- cardboard box with a lid, 6¼" x 6¼" (16 x 16 cm), 4⅜" (11 cm) high
- turquoise Nepal wool felt or similar for the lid, 10⅝" x 10⅝" (27 x 27 cm)
- light blue wool felt for the bottom, 10⅝" x 10⅝" (27 x 27 cm) (adjust measurements to fit your box)
- green-colored ball fringe, 25⅝" (65 cm) long
- sharp tapestry needle with large eye

Pattern appears on p. 115

Mouline Thread

		DMC	Anchor
1	1 turquoise	807	168
2	1 purple	3807	177
3	1 dark blue	796	133
4	1 green	3851	187
5	1 red-orange	350	11
6	1 dark pink	3805	62
7	1 gold	E3821	

Instructions

With a marker, draw the pattern for the top of the lid on the turquoise wool felt. Thread three strands of floss onto a sharp tapestry needle with a large eye. Embroider all the borders marked A using chain stitches (see p. 17), and all the borders marked B using backstitches (see p. 16). The area in the middle of the lid features a trellis with cross-stitches (see p. 19). The border at the bottom of the lid's sides should be embroidered after assembling the lid.

Adjust the size of the lid's wool felt edges to fit the size of your cardboard box. Fold in the corners and stitch them together on the right side. Trim the excess material on the inside. Press the seam allowances apart as much as you can, and sew them onto the felt cover's edges on the inside without letting the stitches show on the outside. Embroider the decorative edge of the border on the bottom of the edges and attach the ball fringe. If possible, sew the edges of the wool felt onto the cardboard edges, so the cover does not slide up and down. You also can use fabric glue for this purpose.

Use the same instructions as above to make the bottom of the box.

Made with Love

You'll love wearing a simple store-bought white dress or blouse if it's decorated with some red hearts and lettering. A few hours of work will transform your mass-produced garment into an eye-catching and unique top or dress.

Materials
- white tunic-length linen blouse or dress
- sharp tapestry needle with large eye

Pattern appears on p. 100

Mouline Thread

		DMC	Anchor
■	2 red	666	46

Instructions

Arrange the different pattern components so they fit your garment. The picture (on the opposite page) shows a garment with red hearts embroidered in satin stitches (see p. 19) on the button band between the buttons and on the edges of the sleeves. The pattern repeats four times around the neck on each side. The heart "Made with love" is embroidered on the pocket. A smaller design is added to the split on the opposite side of the blouse to create a balanced look.

Use a sharp tapestry needle and three strands of floss for the embroidery. You will use stem stitches (see p. 16), satin stitches (see p. 19), and French knots (see p. 18) to embroider the different pattern components.

Sweet Birdie Makeup Bag

You can never have too many small bags or purses. When I go out, I need a place to keep my cell phone, keys, and a credit card. And for a quick touch-up, don't forget to include lipstick, mascara, and a compact!

Materials *finished size about 9½" x 4¾" (24 x 12 cm)*

- 2 pieces needlepoint canvas, such as Fleur de Paris 13 mesh; each square represents a cross-stitch at about 13 count (26 threads). Cut each about 9½" x 4¾" (24 x 12 cm).
- 2 pieces cotton fabric for the lining, each about 9½" x 4¾" (24 x 12 cm), not including allowance
- red zipper, 8" (20.5 cm) long, plus sewing thread to match
- sewing machine with zipper foot
- blunt tapestry needle with large eye

Chart appears below

Mouline Thread

		DMC	Anchor
	12 red	666	46
	1 dark pink	3805	62
	4 light pink	605	1094
	1 peach	352	9
	1 orange	741	304
	1 plum	718	88
	1 light green	954	203
	1 turquoise	807	168
	1 light blue	809	130

Instructions

Sew overcast stitches (see p. 19) around all the edges of the needlepoint canvas to avoid fraying. Cross-stitch the designs on the makeup bag using a blunt tapestry needle with a large eye and six strands of floss. Follow the chart below.

If you think it is too much work to cross-stitch two identical sides, you can substitute one embroidered side with a piece of cotton fabric that complements the design.

Place the front and back sides of the bag together, right sides facing, find the center at the top of the bag on the long side, and mark the location for the zipper. Sew a ¾" (2 cm)–long seam on each side. This is where you'll place the zipper.

Press the seam allowances open on both the front and back pieces. Make sure to press both seam allowances open all the way, even though you have not yet sewn the seams the whole length.

Turn your work right sides out. Pin the zipper in place and attach it using a sewing machine and a zipper foot. Start sewing on the left side a little below the zipper tab. Continue down to the end of the zipper, sew across, and continue up on the opposite side. Stop sewing when you get close to the zipper tab. Leave the needle in the fabric, lift up the presser foot, and wiggle the zipper tab past the foot. Continue to sew across and all the way to the starting point.

With right sides facing, fold the front and back sides back on top of each other, and sew the three remaining sides. Press open the seam allowances and trim the excess at the corners. Make sure to leave the zipper open when you sew the sides together. Turn the bag right side out.

Place the lining pieces together, right sides facing, and sew around the sides and bottom. Press the seam allowances and trim, as needed, at the corners.

With right sides facing, place the lining over the stitched bag. Pin the lining along the zipper and sew, leaving a 4" (10 cm) opening. With the bag right side out, turn your work through the lining's opening and press lightly along the bag's top edge. Overcast stitch the opening closed. Lightly press the bag one more time.

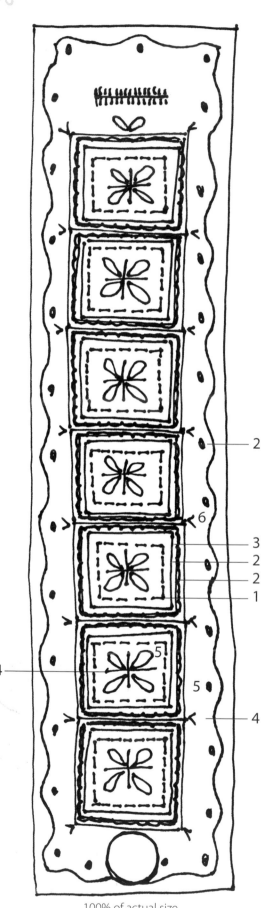

Colorful Glove Cuffs

In Norway, there is a long-standing tradition of wearing glove cuffs when dressing up. These "arm rings" were created with all kinds of ornate, handmade techniques using vividly colored floss or yarns.

Materials
- 2 pieces pink wool felt, each about 4³⁄₈" x 9¼" (11 x 23.5 cm)
- 2 pink buttons
- 2 pieces iron-on interfacing, each about 2" x 9" (5 x 23 cm)
- sharp tapestry needle with large eye

Pattern appears at left

Mouline Thread

		DMC	Anchor
1	1 red-orange	350	11
2	1 dark blue	336	150
3	1 turquoise	3846	1090
4	1 green	703	238
5	1 blue	798	131
6	1 dark red	326	59

Instructions

Transfer the pattern onto the wool felt. Fold the wool felt in two, pin, and sew around the edges with a running stitch (see p. 16). Use a sharp tapestry needle with a large eye and three strands of floss for the stitches. The edging around the cuff is done in a laced running stitch (see p. 17). Use six strands of floss for the lacing part. The squares are embroidered by couching (see p. 17) the floss around the outer square, then sew using chain stitches (see p. 17), and finally couching (see p. 17) two more times. Use six strands of floss when you are couching the inner square in red-orange floss; otherwise use three strands of floss when you sew.

Iron the interfacing onto the back of the cuff. Cut the hole for a buttonhole at one end, and sew tightly spaced blanket stitches (see p. 17) around the hole. Sew a button on at the other end. Repeat the instructions for a second cuff.

100% of actual size

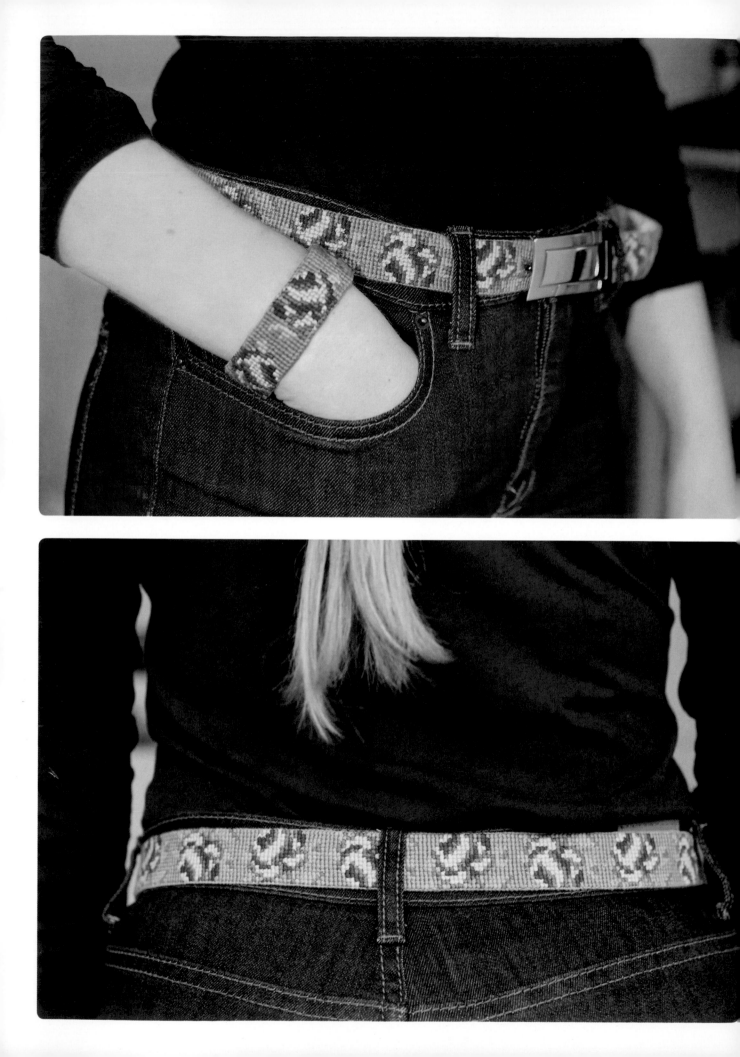

A Belt with Glorious Roses

Roses are red, violets are blue, grapes are sweet, and so are you. These were the words we often wrote in each other's yearbooks when we were teenagers. The pink and magenta colors for roses will never go out of style. Wearing them around the waist enhances any outfit.

Shown here: Size shown is extra large (XL).

Materials *finished size about 1⅛" x 39" (2.7 x 100 cm)*

- ✿ 1 piece needlepoint canvas, such as Fleur de Paris 13 mesh; each square represents a cross-stitch at about 13 count (26 threads). Cut about 2⅛" x 48" (5.4 x 122 cm). (Make sure the measurements fit the intended waist and the belt buckle.)
- ✿ 1 piece cotton fabric for the lining, about 1½" x 48" (3.8 x 122 cm), including allowance
- ✿ belt buckle
- ✿ blunt tapestry needle with large eye

Chart appears at right

Mouline Thread

		DMC	Anchor
	5 turquoise	· 807	168
	1 dark green	701	227
	2 light green	954	203
	3 plum	718	88
	4 dark pink	3805	62
	4 light pink	605	1094

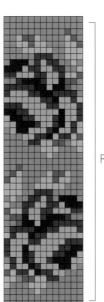

Repeat

Create the buttonholes as shown above.

Instructions

To make the belt, embroider cross-stitches with six strands of floss following the chart shown above right.

Make five buttonholes on the belt opposite the belt buckle end. Place the buttonholes between the roses as shown on the smaller chart (see above right), and use dark green floss to sew tightly spaced blanket sti-ches (see p. 17) around the buttonholes.

Fold any leftover cloth in toward the middle, over-lapping on the back of the belt. Pin and sew the edges together. Using turquoise floss, sew tent stitches (half cross-stiches, see p. 18) along both sides of the belt's edges to hide the canvas edges at the folds. Fold in the lining's seam allowance toward the back side of the lining; pin the lining to the back of the belt, wrong sides together, and overstitch the lining to the belt. Sew overcast stitches around all the raw edges.

Finish by sewing another round of blanket stitches (see p. 17) around the buttonholes and through the belt's three layers.

Handmade Watchband

Variety is fun. If you own a watch that has an interchangeable band, you can exchange your current one for a band that is unique and handmade.

Materials *finished size about 1½" x 8" (4 x 20 cm)*

- ❀ 1 piece needlepoint canvas, such as Fleur de Paris 13 mesh; each square represents a cross-stitch at about 13 Count (26 threads). Cut about 1½" x 8" and adjust the measurements to fit your wrist.
- ❀ use clasp and/or buckle from your watch or see Resources p. 95
- ❀ blunt tapestry needle with large eye

Chart appears below right

Mouline Thread

		DMC	Anchor
	5 turquoise	807	168
	1 dark green	701	227
	2 light green	954	203
	3 plum	718	88
	4 dark pink	3805	62
	4 light pink	605	1094

Instructions

Sew overcast stitches around all the raw edges of the mesh cloth. Use a blunt tapestry needle with a large eye and six strands of floss, and sew following the chart below.

Lightly press the embroidered watchband. Fold the remaining edges toward the back of the watchband and sew them in place. Using three strands of turquoise floss, sew tent stitches (half cross-stitches, see p. 18) along both sides of the band's edges to hide the canvas edges at the folds. Attach the watchband to the watch.

Repeat once

Singing Birdie Napkins

Handmade napkins, enhanced by a small personal touch, make setting a table enjoyable. The birds' shapes for the napkins are the same, but the feather and tail decorations vary, as do the color selections.

Materials

* 4 linen napkins in a natural color, each about 19¾" x 19¾" (50 x 50 cm)
* sharp tapestry needle with large eye

Patterns appears on pp. 102-103

Mouline Thread

		DMC	Anchor
1	1 peach	352	9
2	1 red	666	46
3	1 orange	970	316
4	1 dark pink	3805	62
5	1 purple	3835	98
6	1 blue	334	136
7	1 dark blue	796	133
8	1 ocean green	806	169
9	1 turquoise	3846	1090
10	1 dark green	3814	188
11	1 mint green	3817	203
12	1 neon green	E990	

Instructions:

Transfer the patterns onto the napkins. Embroider the designs using a sharp tapestry needle with a large eye and three strands of floss. The birds' contours are sewn using stem stitches (see p. 16), and the legs are sewn with backstitches (see p. 16). Use satin stitches (see p. 19) for the beaks and eyes, and use long and short stitches (see p. 19) for the breast. Cover the wings with fly stitches (see p. 19) or cross-stitches (see p. 18). Mille fleur stitches (see p. 18) are used for some of the decorations on the feathers.

Robot Pincushion

*If you place several cubes next to each other,
you can make a fun robot. The robot can be used for play
— or you can use it as a pincushion.*

Materials *finished size about 7¾" x 7¾" (20 x 20 cm)*

* 2 pieces needlepoint canvas, such as Fleur de Paris 13 mesh; each square represents a cross-stitch at about 13 Count (26 threads). Cut each about 8" x 8" (20.5 x 20.5 cm).
* rice for filling
* blunt tapestry needle with large eye

Charts appears below

Mouline Thread

		DMC	Anchor
	3 light green	704	256
	3 turquoise	3846	1090
	1 blue	798	131
	1 pink	603	62
	1 red	666	46
	1 white	Blanch	2
	1 orange	741	304

Instructions

Sew overcast stitches around all the raw edges of the needlepoint canvas. Using six strands of floss, sew cross-stitches (see p. 18) following the charts shown below. Do not sew the blue edges before all the squares have been filled in. Cut out the embroidered area allowing for about a ¼" to ³⁄₈" (6 mm to 1 cm)–wide seam allowance. To make the cubes, start by placing side A against A so the seam allowances overlap. Sew cross-stitches (see p. 18) through both layers with blue floss. Next, place side B against B, side C against C, and so forth. Sew through both layers of sides B and C with blue floss. Leave a small opening on the last side so you can pour the rice into the cube before you stitch it closed.

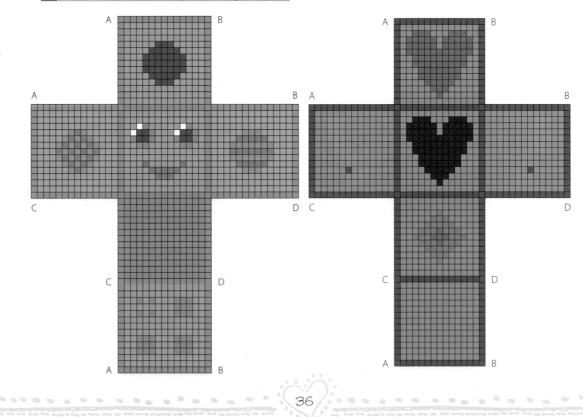

Royal Crown Pincushion

Having a good sense of humor is important; everyday life is boring without it. So, give yourself the privilege of owning your very own royal crown pincushion, one covered in pearls and precious stones. You'll want one of these even if you don't have blue blood in your veins.

Materials

* purple wool felt, 6¼" x 6¼" (16 x 16 cm)
* white wool felt, 3" x 11¾" (7.5 x 30 cm)
* gold rickrack, about 29½" (75 cm) long
* 1 small round package (Camembert cheese box, for example), with about a 3" to 3½" (8 to 9 cm) diameter
* wool roving for filler
* sharp tapestry needle with a large eye
* piece of cardboard cut into 7" (18 cm) circle to use as template

Pattern appears below

Mouline Thread

		DMC	Anchor
■	1 black	310	403
■	1 red	666	46
☐	1 white	Blanc	2
■	1 purple	333	119
☐	1 peach	352	9
■	1 orange	970	316

Instructions

Draw a circle with a 7" (18 cm) diameter on the purple wool felt and cut it out. Baste along the circle's edge using long basting stitches, and place a ball of roving, or another appropriate material, in the center of the circle. Pull on the basting thread, but do not pull it completely closed. Tack the thread to hold it in place. Place the gold rickrack in a cross pattern on the purple felt ball, and along the bottom. Pin the rickrack in place, and attach it to the purple wool felt with French knots (see p. 18). Decorate above the rickrack trim along the bottom of the felt ball by sewing mille fleur stitches (see p. 18) in orange floss and French knots (see p. 18) in red and peach floss.

Fold the sides of the white wool felt lengthwise two times, making three equal layers. Stitch the ends of the felt together to form a ring that will fit around your box. Place one layer of the felt on the inside of the box and two layers on the outside. Decorate the ring of felt with single mille fleur stitches (see p. 18) in black floss, so it gives the illusion of beautiful ermine fur. Place the purple ball in the box and attach the white border to the purple felt ball using the white floss and invisible stitches.

100% of actual size

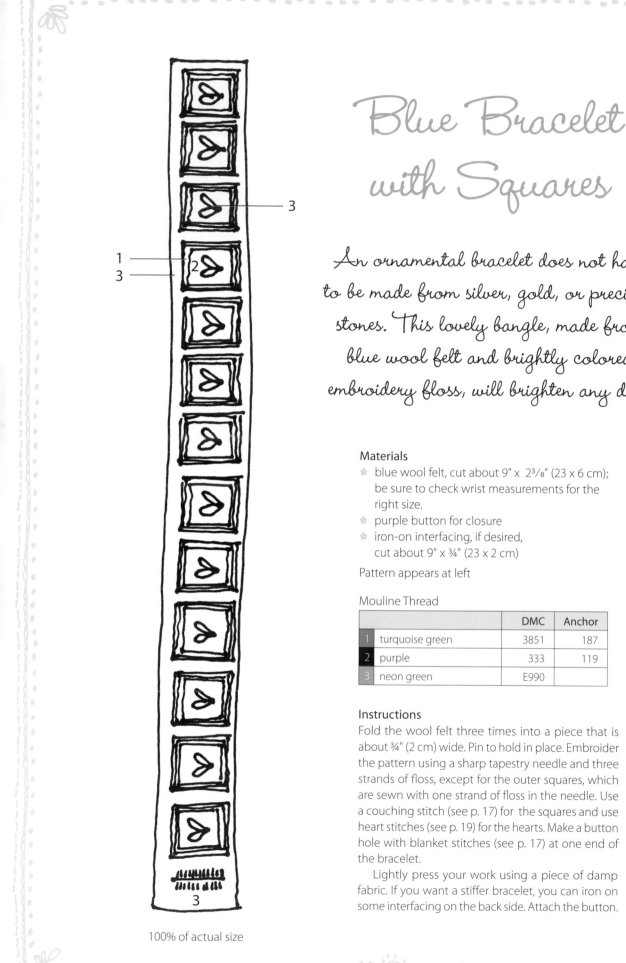

3

1
3

2

3

100% of actual size

Blue Bracelet with Squares

An ornamental bracelet does not have to be made from silver, gold, or precious stones. This lovely bangle, made from blue wool felt and brightly colored embroidery floss, will brighten any day.

Materials
❀ blue wool felt, cut about 9" x 2³⁄₈" (23 x 6 cm); be sure to check wrist measurements for the right size.
❀ purple button for closure
❀ iron-on interfacing, if desired, cut about 9" x ¾" (23 x 2 cm)

Pattern appears at left

Mouline Thread

		DMC	Anchor
1	turquoise green	3851	187
2	purple	333	119
3	neon green	E990	

Instructions
Fold the wool felt three times into a piece that is about ¾" (2 cm) wide. Pin to hold in place. Embroider the pattern using a sharp tapestry needle and three strands of floss, except for the outer squares, which are sewn with one strand of floss in the needle. Use a couching stitch (see p. 17) for the squares and use heart stitches (see p. 19) for the hearts. Make a button hole with blanket stitches (see p. 17) at one end of the bracelet.

Lightly press your work using a piece of damp fabric. If you want a stiffer bracelet, you can iron on some interfacing on the back side. Attach the button.

Roll the Dice

Needlework does not have to be flat! This cube, which has been embroidered on a piece of needlepoint canvas, is very easy to put together.

Materials

* 1 piece needlepoint canvas, such as Fleur de Paris 13 mesh; each square represents a cross-stitch at about 13 count (26 threads). Cut a piece about 8" x 8" (20 x 20 cm).
* rice for filling

Chart appears below

Mouline Thread

		DMC	Anchor
	1 blue	598	1062
	1 pink	899	52
	1 dark pink	602	63
	1 purple	550	102
	1 orange	970	316
	1 light orange	741	304
	1 yellow	444	290
	1 light yellow	726	295

Instructions

Sew overcast stitches (see p. 19) around all the raw edges. Embroider cross-stitches (see p. 19), using six strands of floss, and follow the chart. Hold off embroidering the blue edges until all squares have been completely filled in. Cut out the embroidered part of the canvas leaving about ¼" – ³⁄₈" (0.5 - 1 cm) seam allowance. To assemble the cube, begin by placing A toward A, so that the seam allowances overlap, and sew cross-stitches through both layers using the blue thread. Continue by placing B toward B and C toward C, etc. Leave a small opening in the last side so that you can fill the cube with rice before you close it with a hand stitch.

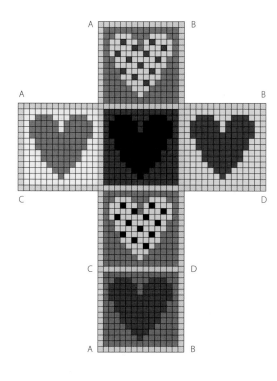

Beetles and Dragonflies

Many people like to collect real insects. Butterflies, dragonflies, beetles, and other insects are caught and placed in a container before they are mounted in display boxes. I think it is easier to embroider them!

Materials
* 3 pieces green linen, about 5⅛" x 5⅛" (13 x 13 cm) (adjust the measurements to fit your frames)
* 3 pieces iron-on interfacing, about 5⅛" x 5⅛" (13 x 13 cm)
* 3 appropriately sized frames
* embroidery hoop
* sharp tapestry needle with large eye

Patterns appear below right

Mouline Thread

		DMC	Anchor
1	2 dark blue	796	133
2	1 dark green	597	188
3	1 light blue	813	140
4	1 silver	E168	

Instructions
Sew overcast stitches around all the raw edges. Use the patterns shown at right to trace the beetles and dragonflies onto your fabric. Use an embroidery hoop, a sharp tapestry needle with a large eye, and three strands of floss when embroidering.

Instructions for embroidering beetles:
1) Use a satin stitch (see p. 19) to fill in the beetle's large body and to create height.
2) Use a satin stitch to embroider in the long or opposite direction.
3) Use a satin stitch to embroider horizontally across the "middle body."
4) Use a satin stitch to embroider the head horizontally.
5) Embroider six legs and two antennae using a backstitch (see p. 16).
6) Divide the body into two using the silver thread, and with one strand of floss, make the eyes with French knots (see p. 18).

Instructions for embroidering dragonflies:
1) To make stripes, use a satin stitch (see p. 19) to embroider across the body with one dark color and one light color of floss.
2) Embroider a few dark-colored floss stitches on the wings.
3) With the main color of floss, fill in the wings using long and short stitches (see p. 19).
4) Use one strand of a lighter floss color and short stitches to fill in the spaces between the stitches on the wings.

Lightly press your work and iron the interfacing onto the back.
Place the embroideries in the frames without glass.

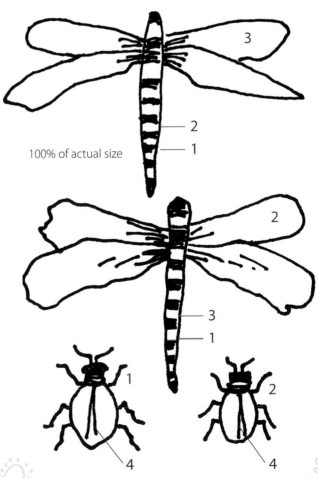

100% of actual size

Happy Birds Linen Pillow

This happy pillow will create a celebration of colors on your sofa or chair. It will brighten any interior, and it is even very comfortable to lean against when you are going to be sitting for a long time.

Materials

* 2 pieces green linen 20½" x 20½" (52 x 52 cm), and 2 additional pieces 12¼" x 12¼" (31 x 31 cm)
* 18" (45.5 cm) long green zipper
* 20" (51 cm)–long bolster pillow insert
* sharp tapestry needle with large eye
* sewing machine with zipper foot and matching thread

Pattern appears on pp. 124-125

Mouline Thread

		DMC	Anchor
1	peach	352	9
2	red	666	46
3	orange	970	316
4	dark pink	3805	62
5	purple	3835	98
6	blue	334	136
7	dark blue	796	133
8	ocean green	806	169
9	turquoise	3846	1090
10	dark green	3814	188
11	mint	3817	203
12	neon green	E990	

Instructions

Sew overcast stitches around all of the linen's raw edges. For placement of the birds on the pillow, trace the pattern provided on pp. 124-125, onto the fabric. For color details, refer to pp. 102-103 (the birds are embroidered in the same way). Use a sharp tapestry needle and three strands of floss for the bird embroideries.

Cut out two circles with a 12¼" (31 cm) diameter (verify the size by measuring your pillow insert) from the two smaller linen pieces. Sew overcast stitches around all the raw edges.

Place the large, embroidered linen piece so the two short ends match up and create a "roll." Find the middle of the short ends and mark the location for the zipper. Place the short ends right sides together, pin, and sew the seams using a 1¼" (3.2 cm) seam allowance on each side of the zipper. Leave the space for the zipper open. Press all the seam allowances open, including the zipper opening.

Turn the fabric embroidered side out, and pin the zipper in place. Using a sewing machine and a zipper foot, sew the zipper to the zipper opening. Start sewing on the left side of the opening, a little past the zipper tab. Continue sewing to the end of the zipper, across the zipper, and up the other side. Stop when you are close to the zipper tab. Leave the sewing machine needle in the fabric, raise the zipper foot, and move the tab past the sewing machine foot. Finish sewing to the top of the zipper and across, finishing where you started.

With the right sides together, pin the round ends to the "roll." Using a ½" (1.3 cm) seam allowance and a sewing machine, sew the seams. Press the seam allowances open. Turn the pillow cover inside out and insert the bolster pillow insert into the cover.

All You Need Is Love

A heart shape is the most used symbol today. It may be popular because it is believed to be a symbol of positive expression. The heart stands for everything we dream of, everything we associate with a good life — love, goodness, friendship, and warmth.

Materials

- 1 piece white linen, about 11" x 14" (28 x 35.5 cm)
- canvas stretcher bars to fit linen
- sharp tapestry needle with large eye

Pattern appears on p. 127

Mouline Thread

		DMC	Anchor
	2 red	666	46
	1 plum	817	13
	1 dark pink	718	88
	1 pink	603	62
	1 light pink	605	1094
	1 purple	550	102
	1 light purple	3607	87
	1 orange	741	304

Instructions

Sew overcast stitches around all the raw edges of the linen. Trace the pattern found on p. 127 and transfer it (see transferring patterns on p. 14) to the fabric. Embroider all of the designs with a sharp tapestry needle and three strands of floss, except for the horizontal lines, which are embroidered with one strand of floss. Following the grain of the fabric's weave, embroider the lines using backstitches (see p. 16) and red floss. The text has been embroidered with stem stitches (see p. 16), and the heart with French knots (see p. 18) and irregular running stitches (see p. 16). Use the darkest floss color for only a few stitches. The running stitches are primarily embroidered with pink and light pink floss. The other floss colors are equally distributed.

Lightly press your embroidery. Attach your embroidery to a stretched canvas frame, making sure it is stretched equally on all sides. Stretch the embroidery in one direction first, and then stretch it in the other direction. Always start stretching in the middle of one side, and work your way to the corners. Sew threads into the embroidered linen on the back of the canvas about ⅜" (1 cm) apart.

Make sure to stitch the lines across from side to side.

All you need is love, all you
need is love, all you need is
love, love, love is all you need.
I ♥ Your Style
Amanda Brooks
BOBBI BROWN MAKEUP MANUAL
VOGUE
SEPTEMBER 2012
VOGUE
SEPTEMBER 2009
VOGUE
SEPTEMBER 2010

TRIKOTASJE
UNDERTØY
STRØMPER

Table Runner Decorated with Wild Parsley

Spread summer all over your table! Simple, stylized wild parsley on a blue background will remind you of summers past, or spark anticipations of the summer to come — sunshine, mosquito bites, wild strawberries, late nights, swimming in the ocean . . .

Materials
★ blue linen table runner, about 19¾" x 59" (50 x 150 cm) (or whatever size fits your table)
★ sharp tapestry needle with large eye

Pattern appears on pp. 120-123

Mouline Thread

		DMC	Anchor
1	1 ecru	543	933
2	1 off-white	3033	391
3	1 white	3865	2
4	1 gray	3024	213
5	1 gray-green	3813	875

Instructions
Trace the pattern (see pp. 120-123). Distribute the different groups of flower patterns on your runner so they make a balanced composition. Embroider the wild parsley's stems, knots, and straws using a sharp tapestry needle and three strands of floss.

The "parachute" seedpod is embroidered with a single strand of floss.

For the Math Lover

Cool T-shirts are popular, especially among the younger generation. You might as well make them yourself. This is designed for a young man who is above average and very interested in math.

Materials
* adult size blue T-shirt
* sharp tapestry needle with large eye

Pattern appears on pp. 104-105

Mouline Thread

		DMC	Anchor
	1 light blue	813	161
	1 light green	959	185

Instructions

Embroider the design using a sharp tapestry needle and three strands of floss.

Transfer the pattern onto the T-shirt (see pp. 104-105). Place the office chair a little to the left of the middle on the shirt, and place the math problems and formulas around it. Embroider the design using stem stitches (see p. 16). The chair is embroidered in light blue floss, and the math problems/formulas are embroidered in light green floss.

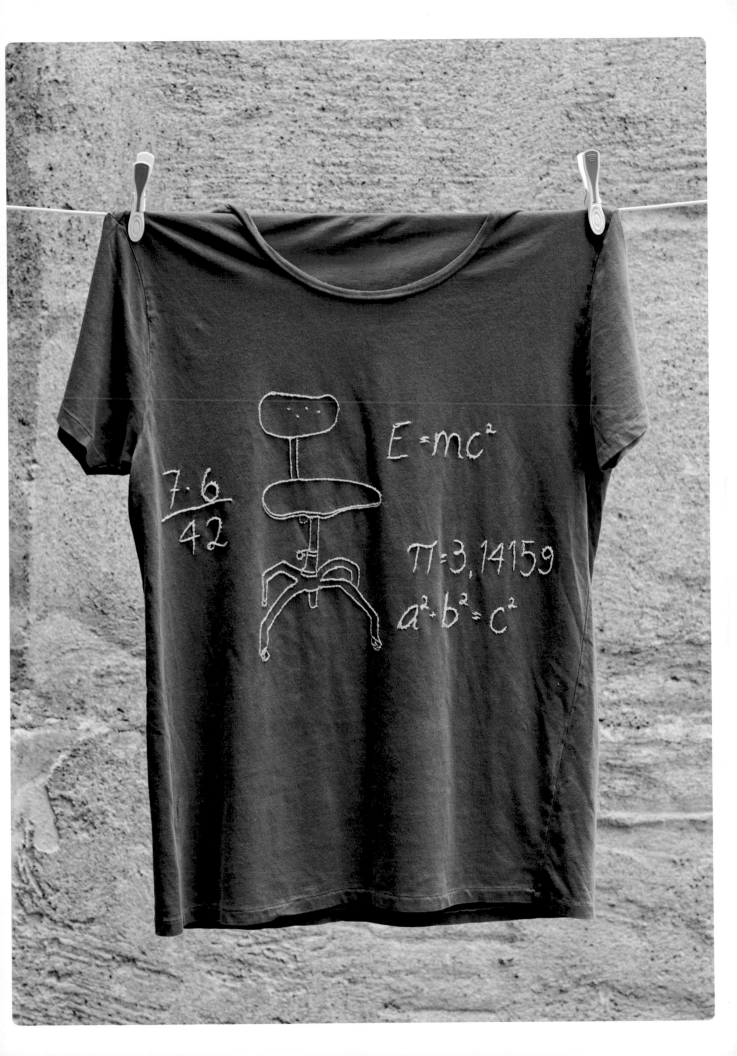

A Trolley Car

It has been 120 years since Oslo, Norway, got its first trolley car. Many people consider the light blue trolley to be much more than a means of transportation. This sentiment also exists in many other cities. What would the cityscapes of San Francisco, Lisbon, Stockholm, and Prague be without their wagons on rails?

Materials

- fabric with a muted pattern cut into a circle with a 13" (33 cm) diameter
- iron-on interfacing, cut into a circle with a 13" (33 cm) diameter
- embroidery hoop about 10¼" (26 cm) in diameter
- sharp tapestry needle with large eye

Pattern appears on p. 106

Mouline Thread

		DMC	Anchor
	1 light blue	809	130

Instructions:

Sew overcast stitches around all the raw edges. Transfer the pattern onto the fabric (see p. 14), then place the fabric in the embroidery hoop. Embroider the design using a sharp tapestry needle and three strands of floss. Use stem stitches (see p. 16), backstitches (see p. 16), satin stitches (see p. 19), and couching (see p. 17) to embroider the image.

Remove your embroidery from the hoop and lightly press it from the back. Iron on the interfacing. Frame the finished piece using the embroidery hoop. Sew basting stitches all around the edges of the embroidery fabric and tighten the stitches by pulling on the thread after you have placed the embroidery back in the hoop. Fasten off the basting thread.

Drawstring Canvas Bag with Beetles and Dragonflies

It is impossible to have too many bags! Sometimes we need large bags, and sometimes we need small ones. We must also make sure the bag's colors and style match the outfit we are wearing.

Materials

* 2 pieces linen, such as Rustic weight (7.1 oz) linen, see Resources, p. 95, cut one piece 9¾" x 11" (25 x 28 cm), and the other piece a circle with a 6¼" (16 cm) diameter, plus allowance
* 2 pieces light blue cotton fabric for the lining, one piece 10⅝" x 19" (27 x 48 cm), and the other piece a circle with a 6¼" (16 cm) diameter, plus allowance
* round cord, 17¾" (45 cm) long and about ¼" (6 mm) in diameter
* light blue round cord, 43¼" (110 cm) long and ⅛" (3 mm) in diameter
* embroidery hoop
* sharp tapestry needle with large eye
* sewing machine with matching thread

Pattern appears on pp. 116-117

Mouline Thread

		DMC	Anchor
1	1 dark blue	796	133
2	1 medium blue	3838	1030
3	1 blue	312	178
4	1 medium green	3851	187
5	1 light green	954	203
6	1 light blue	813	140
7	1 dark green	3814	188
8	1 silver	E168	

Instructions

Sew overcast stitches around all the raw edges. Using the pattern on pp. 116-117, trace the beetles and dragonflies (see p. 14 for transferring patterns) onto the canvas. Use an embroidery hoop, sharp tapestry needle, and three strands of floss when embroidering.

Instructions for embroidering beetles:

1) Use a satin stitch (see p. 19) to fill in the beetle's large body and to create height.
2) Use a satin stitch to embroider in the long or opposite direction.
3) Use a satin stitch to embroider horizontally across the "middle body." *See stitching guide at the top of p. 59.*

4) Use a satin stitch to embroider the head in the opposite direction as the body.
5) Embroider six legs and two antennae using a backstitch (see p. 16).
6) Use one strand of dark green floss to decorate the body.
7) Using one strand of silver floss divide the lower body in two and make French knots (see p. 18) for the eyes.

Instructions for embroidering dragonflies:

1) Use a satin stitch (see p. 19) to embroider stripes across the dragonfly's body using one dark color and one light color of floss.
2) Sew a few dark stitches on the wings.
3) Fill in the wings using long and short stitches (see p. 19).

Lightly press the embroidery. Place the two embroidered pieces together, right sides facing, and stitch the sides together in this way: sew 1¾" (4.5 cm) down from the top, leave a ⅝" (1.5 cm) opening, and sew the remaining 8⅝" (22 cm) side seam to the end. Lightly press the seam allowances open. Pin the bottom of the bag in place and sew. Fold down the bottom seam allowances, and place the ¼" (6 mm) diameter cord along the bottom edge. Hand stitch the cord in place.

Sew the lining, right sides together, into a cylinder, but leave a 4" (10 cm) opening in the middle. Lightly press the seam allowances open. Pin the bottom of the bag, right sides facing, to the cylinder, and sew.

Place the lining on top of the embroidered bag with right sides facing. Pin the top seam edges together and sew along the seam lines. Turn your work right side out through the opening in the lining, and lightly press the upper edge. Sew the opening in the lining closed. Sew the seams about 1" (2.5 cm) and 1¾" (4.5 cm) from the top edge of the bag. Pull the two cords, about 21⅝" (55 cm) long, through the tubes created by the seams. The cords will act as handles for your bag.

Boogie-Woogie Beetle Purse

Some people think beetles look frightening, yet many beetles
have exotic exteriors and sheaths that feature the most beautiful
colors. The beetles I've drawn here are completely safe,
and they are fun to embroider!

58

Materials

* ⭐ 2 pieces linen, such as Rustic weight (7.1 oz), see Resources, p. 95. Cut the fabric to a size that will work with the purse clasp, about 5¾" x 7" (14.5 x 18 cm), plus allowance.
* ⭐ 2 pieces patterned cotton fabric for lining. Cut each to match the measurement for the linen. 5¾" x 7" (14.5 x 18 cm), plus allowance
* ⭐ purse clasp (with "frame")
* ⭐ embroidery hoop
* ⭐ sharp tapestry needle with large eye
* ⭐ sewing machine and matching thread

Pattern appears below right

Mouline Thread

		DMC	Anchor
⬛	2 dark blue	796	133
⬛	1 turquoise	807	168
⬜	1 silver	E168	

Instructions

Sew overcast stitches around all the raw edges. Trace the beetle patterns shown below right and transfer them onto the fabric. Use an embroidery hoop, a sharp tapestry needle, and three strands of floss when embroidering the beetles.

1) Use a satin stitch (see p. 19) and embroider across the beetle's large body to fill it in and to create height.
2) Use a satin stitch and embroider in the long direction, or opposite direction.
3) Use a satin stitch to embroider horizontally across the "middle body."
4) Use a satin stitch to embroider the head in the opposite direction as the rest of the body.
5) Embroider six legs and two antennae using a backstitch (see p. 16).
6) Using one strand of floss, decorate the body using turquoise.
7) Using one strand of silver floss, divide the lower body in two. Make the eyes with French knots (see p. 18).

Place the canvas fabric pieces together, right sides facing, and sew the sides and bottom together along the seam lines. Press the seam allowances open. Sew and attach the lining in the same manner.

With right sides facing, slip the lining over the canvas purse. Sew the seams together at the top of the purse (where you will attach the clasp to the purse). Be sure to leave an opening of about 4" (10 cm) on one side. Press the seam allowances open, and turn the purse right side out. Sew the opening closed. Place the fabric into the purse clasp and sew the purse to the clasp using blanket stitches (see p. 17). You can also attach the purse to the clasp by using a sharp tapestry needle and six strands of floss.

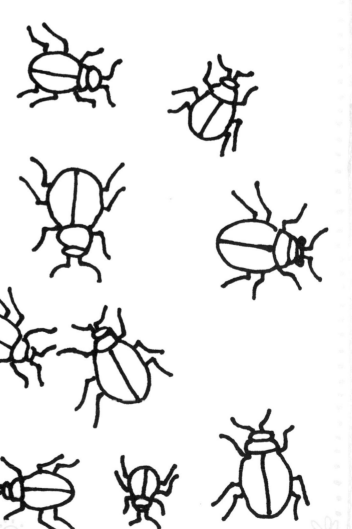

A Square Linen Tablecloth with Blue Triangles

Sashiko, which means little stabs, is a Japanese embroidery technique that was originally used to repair textiles. Traditionally, a running stitch in white thread is used to embroider on an indigo-colored fabric. Here, we are inspired to embroider a tablecloth with a variegated, indigo-colored thread on white linen.

Materials
* square linen tablecloth, about 43¾" x 43¾" (111 x 111 cm), or whatever size fits your table

Yarn
* about 4 oz (120 g) Delicato from Prism Yarns (100% Tencel), hand dyed/multicolored, variegated blue Plum Dandy
  or: about 8 skeins DMC blue Mouline thread, no. 93 or 121

Pattern appears below

Instructions
Locate the center of each side of the tablecloth in order to center the triangle patterns and place the pattern completely on the edge of the fabric. Transfer the pattern (see p. 14) onto the tablecloth. The tablecloth shown has room for seven triangles on each of the four sides. You can easily adapt the pattern to fit rectangular and square tablecloths of all sizes. Since the ink from the marker you use to draw the triangles on the tablecloth will disappear before you may have finished the work, it makes sense to sew around the drawn triangles with basting stitches. Doing this will preserve the outline of the triangles even after the ink has disappeared. After you have embroidered the triangles, you can easily pull out the basting stitches.

The triangles are filled with uneven running stitches (see p. 16), but they are stitched following the grain of the weave toward the middle of the tablecloth. It is important to pay careful attention to the triangles' edges, so they are formal and precise.

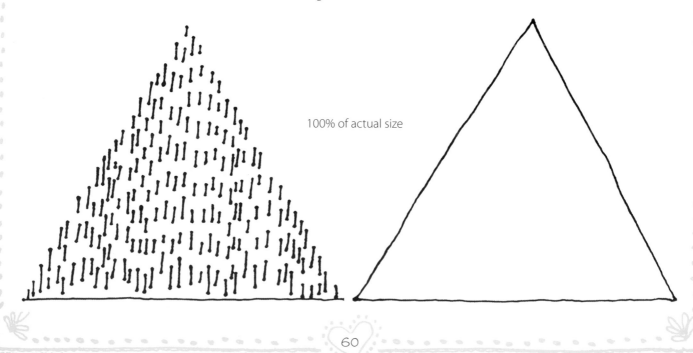

100% of actual size

A Dachshund in a Sweater

Look, the dog is wagging its tail! It is also wearing a sweater — a sweater with stripes of many colors. Have you ever seen a dog like this before?

Materials

✿ child size light green T-shirt
✿ sharp tapestry needle with large eye

Pattern appears on p. 111

Instructions

Transfer the pattern (see p. 14) to the T-shirt and embroider using three strands of floss for all stitches. Use stem stitches (see p. 16), satin stitches (see p. 19), running stitches (see p. 16), and fly stitches (see p. 19).

Mouline Thread

		DMC	Anchor
1	1 purple	550	102
2	1 blue	995	142
3	1 pink	603	62
4	1 yellow	444	290
5	1 turquoise	3845	1089
6	1 green	3851	187
7	1 light purple	3607	87
8	1 red	666	46
9	1 ocean green	806	169
10	1 orange	741	304
11	1 light green	704	256

Princess Dress with Wild Strawberries

Most little princesses love pink dresses. Decorate this one with borders that bring to mind the pleasures of summer — embroidered grass, dancing flowers, and wild strawberries on the bottom hem, with a wreath of flower buds at the neck.

Materials
- child size pink-and-white striped dress, or similar
- sharp tapestry needle with large eye

Pattern appears on pp. 108-109

Mouline Thread

		DMC	Anchor
1	1 dark pink	601	57
2	1 light pink	894	27
3	1 pink	3833	55
4	1 green	702	226
5	2 red	666	46
6	1 gold	E3821	

Instructions
Transfer the pattern onto the dress about ¾" (2 cm) above the bottom of the hem. The grass is embroidered using uneven running stitches (see p. 16); the flowers using mille fleur stitches (see p. 18) and French knots (see p. 18). The strawberries are embroidered using satin stitches (see p. 19) and couching (see p. 17), with mille fleur stitches for the leaves. The flower bud wreath around the neck is embroidered using French knots and a few mille fleur stitches for the leaves.

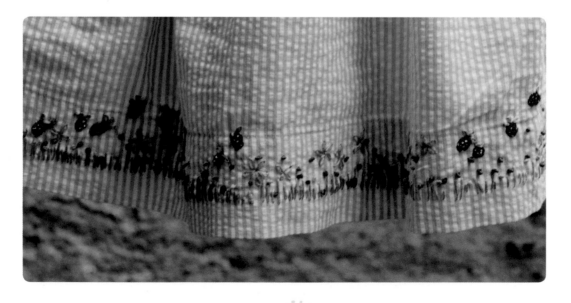

Three Colorful Bracelets

Flowers have always been popular decorative motifs, but are you in the mood to try something a little different? I offer traditional flowers as well as stylized ladybugs and some fun pastel-colored squares that bring a modern geometric look.

Bracelet with Pastel Squares:

Materials *finished size about 1" x 7" (2.6 x 18 cm)*

* 1 piece needlepoint canvas, such as Fleur de Paris 13 mesh; each square represents a cross-stitch at about 13 count (26 threads). Cut piece about 1" x 7⅛" (2.6 x 18 cm), including allowance.
* sharp tapestry needle with large eye

Moulin Thread

		DMC	Anchor
	1 light blue	813	161
	1 light yellow	3819	278
	1 light pink	605	1094
	1 light green	959	185
	1 yellow	444	290
	1 pink	3806	52
	1 blue	598	1062

Repeat

Bracelet with Flowers:

Materials *finished size about ⅞" x 6½" (2.2 x 16.5 cm)*

* 1 piece needlepoint canvas, such as Fleur de Paris 13 mesh; each square represents a cross-stitch at about 13 count (26 threads). Cut piece about 1" x 7⅛" (2.6 x 18 cm), including allowance.
* sharp tapestry needle with large eye

Moulin Thread

		DMC	Anchor
	1 dark pink 1	3805	62
	1 dark pink 2	602	63
	1 light pink	604	55
	1 very light pink	963	48
	1 green	3851	187
	1 light green	704	256

Repeat

Bracelet with Ladybugs:

Materials *finished size about 1" x 7" (2.6 x 18 cm)*

* 1 piece needlepoint canvas, such as Fleur de Paris 13 mesh; each square represents a cross-stitch at about 13 count (26 threads). Cut piece about 1" x 7⅛" (2.6 x 18 cm), including allowance.
* sharp tapestry needle with large eye

Moulin Thread

		DMC	Anchor
	1 red	666	46
	1 black	310	403
	1 light pink	605	1094

Repeat

Instructions

Following the charts on p. 66, embroider cross-stitches with a blunt tapestry needle and six strands of floss. For each ladybug, divide the red body into two parts by sewing backstitches (see p. 16) in black floss down the middle of the body. Lightly press your embroidery. Fold the edges in toward the back of the bracelet, stitch the edges in place. Sew overcast stitches (see p. 19) around all raw edges.

Festive Suspenders

Recently, manufacturers of men's pants returned to a time-honored trend to include buttons on the waistband of their pants. This upbeat suspender design is perfect for ready-made pants with buttons, or add them to a favorite pair of denim jeans or dress pants.

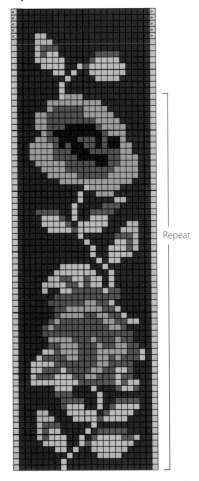

Repeat

Materials *finished size about 2" x 31½" (5 x 80 cm), not including leather pieces*

❋ 2 pieces needlepoint canvas, such as Fleur de Paris 13 mesh; each square represents a cross-stitch at about 13 count (26 threads). Cut each about 4¾" x 33" (12 x 84 cm), and adjust the measurements to fit the person; take into account the leather drop ends and ears you will use to make the suspenders.

❋ 2 pieces cotton fabric with small flower print for the lining, each about 2¾" x 32¼" (7 x 82 cm)

❋ leather drop ends with leather ears for the button end of the suspenders

❋ sharp tapestry needle with large eye

(See Resources on p. 95 for more info.)

Chart appears at right

Yarn

	3.5 oz (100 g) Dale Baby Wool	Bright Pink 4516
	3.5 oz (100 g) Rauma Baby Panda	Tomato Red 18
	1.75 oz (50 g) Dale Baby Wool	Dark Red 4018
	1.75 oz (50 g) Dale Baby Wool	Pink 4504
	1.75 oz (50 g) Rauma Baby Panda	Orange 60
	1.75 oz (50 g) Dale Baby Wool	Olive 2231
	1.75 oz (50 g) Rauma Baby Panda	Green 95
	1.75 oz (50 g) Rauma Baby Panda	Light Turquoise 48

Instructions

Sew overcast stitches around all the raw edges of the canvas. Embroider the design using cross-stitches or half cross-stitches (see p. 18), also known as tent stitches, following the chart above right. Wait until the very end before sewing tent stitches along the edge on both sides of the suspenders.

Fold in the leftover canvas toward the back of the suspenders and overlap the seams. Pin and stitch the seams in place by hand. The edge of each side of the suspenders is sewn using tent stitches to hide the raw, folded canvas edge. Use a double strand of wool for this. Fasten the suspenders to the leather drop ends. Fold in the edges of the lining, pin, and hand stitch the lining to the back of the suspenders. Sew tent stitches toward the left on the left side and toward the right on the right side.

Party Corset with Stylized Roses

Many of the national costumes of Norway (bunad) proudly display the enormous joy of embellishment that Norwegians love. This summertime party corset was inspired by some colorful roses on a traditional folk costume from Hallingdal, Norway.

Materials

* white cotton corset or similar party top (see Resources on p. 95)
* sharp tapestry needle with large eye

Pattern appears on pp. 98-99

Mouline Thread

		DMC	Anchor
1	1 very light pink	963	73
2	2 light pink 1	605	1094
3	1 light pink 2	604	55
4	1 dark pink	3805	62
5	1 peach	352	9
	1 red	666	46
7	1 light blue	813	161
8	1 light green	954	203

Instructions

Trace the pattern (see p. 14), and adjust it to fit the top you have selected. Embroider the designs shown on the pattern using a sharp tapestry needle with three strands of floss. The photograph of the finished corset has metal underwire at the bustline; satin stitches (see p. 19) emphasize the corset's top. Embroider the stylized roses shown by using satin stitches (see p. 19) and stem stitches (see p. 16).

Crocodile Loves Cupcakes

With a few stitches, transform a simple little cotton top into a fun fairy-tale garment for a child (or adult, for that matter!). This crocodile will never get enough cupcakes, and whenever he has a chance, he will eat them for breakfast, lunch, and dinner!

Materials
* child size pink cotton T-shirt with long sleeves
* sharp tapestry needle with large eye

Pattern appears on p. 119

Mouline Thread

		DMC	Anchor
1	1 green	704	256
2	1 turquoise	807	168
3	1 blue	792	941
4	1 red	666	46
5	1 very light pink	963	48
6	1 flesh	758	868

Instructions

Transfer the pattern (see p. 14) onto the T-shirt so the stack of cupcakes is on the right-hand side when viewing the T-shirt from the front. The crocodile is so long that he wraps around and continues on to the back of the shirt. How far he extends is determined by the shirt's size. If it's smaller than a small (size 7 years), the pattern should be reduced in size to fit the shirt. Embroider the design using a sharp tapestry needle and three strands of floss.

Embroider the crocodile and the cupcake liners using stem stitches (see p. 16). The cake part of the cupcake, the frosting, berries, and the crocodile's eyes are embroidered using satin stitches (see p. 19).

Ladybug Sneakers

Decorate your shoes just a little — and they will stand out a lot. This is very useful in a kindergarten class where many children have the same types of shoes.

Materials

- ★ one pair child size pink canvas sneakers
- ★ sharp tapestry needle with large eye (leather needle optional)

Pattern appears below

Mouline Thread

		DMC	Anchor
■	1 red	666	46
■	1 black	310	406

Instructions

Embroider the shoes using a sharp tapestry needle and three strands of floss. Use a leather needle for embroidering on the canvas if it gets too difficult to sew through the fabric with a tapestry needle, but be careful not to tear the canvas.

Transfer the pattern (see p. 14) onto the shoes using a marker with disappearing ink. Embroider the ladybugs using red floss and satin stitches (see p. 19) as shown. Use backstitches (see p. 16) and black floss to embroider the line in the middle of the ladybug's body and legs. The black dots on the ladybug's body are sewn using small cross-stitches (see p. 18) and black floss.

100% of actual size

A Caged Bird Sings!

This purse clasp is shaped like a birdcage. So, inside I have placed a singing bird that will magically bring forth the most beautiful melody to liven your day.

Materials

* 2 pieces needlepoint canvas, such as Fleur de Paris 13 mesh; each square represents a cross-stitch at about 13 count (26 threads). Cut each about 5½" x 6¾" (14 x 17 cm).
* 2 pieces cotton fabric for lining, each about 5½" x 6¾" (14 x 17 cm)
* 6" purse clasp (see Resources p. 95)
* blunt tapestry needle with large eye

Charts appear below

Mouline Thread

		DMC	Anchor
	6 purple	333	119
	1 plum	718	88
	1 dark pink	3805	62
	1 peach	352	9
	1 turquoise	3845	1089
	3 green	704	256
	1 orange	741	304
	2 silver	E168	

Instructions

Sew overcast stitches around all the raw edges. Embroider the birds, using cross-stitches, following the chart shown below using a blunt tapestry needle and six strands of floss.

Cut the needlepoint canvas pieces so they fit the purse clasp. Place the embroidered pieces together, right sides facing, and sew the sides and the bottom purse seams. Press the seam allowances open. Sew the lining in the same way.

Place the lining on top of the embroidered purse, right sides facing, and sew the pieces together at the top where the clasp will be attached, but leave an opening of about 4" (10 cm) on one side. Press the seam allowances open, and turn the purse right side out. Sew the opening closed. Place the embroidered purse into the clasp, and hand stich it to the clasp. Use buttonhole thread, or six strands of floss, to attach the purse to the clasp.

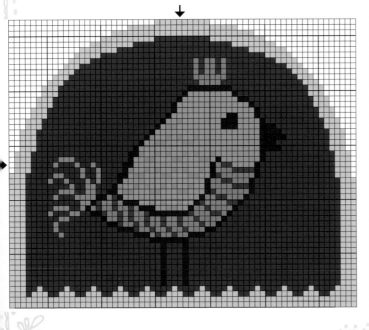
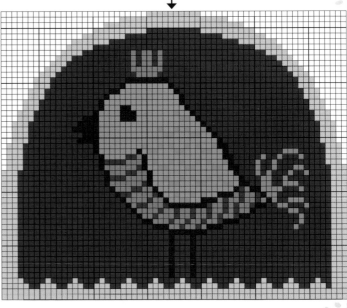

Embroidered Zipper Bag

Cross-stitches embroidered on needlepoint canvas make a very sturdy and long-lasting purse. This is the reason why women have, for more than 100 years, made purses and wallets using these materials.

Materials

- 2 pieces needlepoint canvas, such as Fleur de Paris 13 mesh; each square reprsents a cross-stitch at about 13 count (26 threads). Cut each about 4¾" x 9½" (12 x 24 cm).
- 2 pieces cotton fabric for lining, each about 4¾" x 9½" (12 x 24 cm)
- 8" (20.5 cm)–long red zipper
- blunt tapestry needle with large eye
- sewing machine with zipper foot and matching thread

Chart appears below

Mouline Thread

		DMC	Anchor
	10 red	666	46
	4 dark pink	3805	62
	1 light pink	605	1094
	1 peach	352	9
	1 orange	741	304
	1 plum	718	88
	1 light green	954	203
	1 light blue	813	140
	1 turquoise	807	168

Instructions

Sew overcast stitches around all the raw edges. Embroider, using cross-stitches, the design using a blunt tapestry needle with six strands of floss following the chart below.

If you decide it is too much work to embroider both sides of the purse, replace the back with a cotton fabric that matches the embroidered side. Place the embroidered pieces together, right sides facing. Find the middle on the long side and mark the location for the zipper. Sew about a ¾" (2 cm)–long seam on each side of the zipper, leaving an opening in the middle for the zipper. Press all seam allowances open, including the zipper opening.

Turn your work right side out, pin the zipper in place, and sew. Start sewing on the left side of the zipper a little beyond the zipper tab, and continue sewing down to the end of the zipper. Sew across the zipper and up the right side toward the zipper tab. Stop sewing when you are almost at the zipper tab. Leave the needle in the fabric, raise the zipper foot, and pull the zipper tab beyond the foot. Continue to sew to the top of the zipper. Sew across the zipper, and stop sewing when you have returned to where you started.

Place the purse's front and back pieces together, right sides facing. Make sure the zipper is open. Sew the side seams and bottom seams of the purse together. Press the seam allowances open, and trim the seams at the corners. Turn the purse right side out.

Place the two pieces of lining together, right sides facing, and sew the side seams and the bottom seams together. Press the seam allowances open, and trim the corner seams.

Place the lining over the embroidered purse, right sides facing. Pin the lining to the zipper and sew, making sure to leave a 4" (10 cm)–long opening. Turn the purse right side out through the lining's opening, and lightly press the lining along the zipper. Sew the opening closed.

Happy Birthday Banner

Make something special for the birthday celebrations in your home. Celebrate with a handmade happy birthday banner. Hang it outside or inside every time someone in your family has a birthday. It's great whether you are decorating for a children's party or celebrating Dad's birthday. It's a perfect way to use your stash of leftover cotton fabric and floss!

Materials

* cotton fabrics in different colors cut according to the pattern with a ¼" (6 mm) seam allowance
* 2 pieces 8¾" x 11½" (22 x 29 cm) fabric for each pendant (fabric should be a solid color or have a very faint pattern, so the embroidered letters are easy to read).
* cord for hanging, about 4.8 yds (4.4 m) long
* sharp tapestry needle with large eye

Patterns appear on pp. 112-114

Instructions

Sew overcast stitches around all the raw edges. Trace the letter patterns, draw your own, or use a stencil to draw the letters on the fabric pendants. Fill in the letters by embroidering the stitches as suggested on the patterns (see pp. 112-113). Embroider the letters using a sharp tapestry needle and three strands of floss.

Place the cotton fabric pendants that belong together on top of each other (one with an embroidered letter and the other one without), right sides facing. Pin, sew the sides, and sew a 2" (5 cm)–long seam on each side at the top of the pendant. Press the seam allowances open and trim the corner seams. Turn the pendant right side out and stitch the top opening closed. Fold down the top to create a pocket for the cord, pin the seam enclosing the cord, and sew.

Pull the cord through the cord pockets when all the pendants are complete. Stitch the pendants in place on the cord so they do not slip. Leave an open space the size of a pendant between "Happy" and "Birthday."

Mouline Thread

		DMC	Anchor
H			
1	1 purple	3807	122
2	1 dark green	3814	188
3	1 light green	954	203
A			
4	1 plum	718	89
5	1 dark pink 1	602	63
P			
6	1 turquoise 1	3845	1089
7	1 green 1	703	238
P			
8	1 pink	603	62
9	1 red	666	46
10	1 orange	741	304
11	1 dark pink 2	917	088
Y			
12	1 blue	995	142
13	1 dark green	701	227
B			
14	1 yellow	444	290
15	1 light pink	604	55
I			
16	1 orange	741	304
R			
17	1 dark blue	796	133
8	1 pink*	603	62
T			
6	1 turquoise 1*	3845	1089
18	1 turquoise 2	3846	1090
19	1 light blue	809	130
20	1 green 2	3851	187
21	1 blue-green	3753	1031
22	1 purple	333	119
H			
23	1 dark red	817	13
15	1 light pink*	604	55
24	1 salmon	3801	35
D			
25	1 light yellow	726	295
A			
23	1 dark red*	817	13
Y			
17	1 dark blue*	796	133

*Use the same skein as listed above.

Birthday Crown

We love traditions. That is why children should have their own birthday crown to help them celebrate when their birthday comes along. All that you need are a few stitches on a piece of wool felt. You may want to choose different colors for each child.

Materials

* 1 piece of dark blue wool felt, about 3¼" x 24¾" (8.5 x 63 cm)
* 1 piece of light blue wool felt, about 4" x 24¾" (10 x 63 cm)
* iron-on stiff interfacing, about 3¼" x 24¾" (8.5 x 63 cm)
* pinking shears
* sharp tapestry needle with large eye
* 3 red buttons

Pattern appears on p. 126

Mouline Thread

		DMC	Anchor
1	1 turquoise	3845	1089
2	1 red	666	46
3	1 orange	741	304
4	1 neon green	E990	

Instructions

Trace the patterns (see p. 14) for the dark blue and the light blue crown onto the different wool felts and cut them out. Use pinking shears to cut a zigzag edge at the bottom of the light blue crown. Pin the two crowns together so the light blue one is visible all around the dark blue crown's edges. Sew all around the crowns using running stitches (see p. 16) as shown on the pattern (see p. 126). Remove the pins, and continue to decorate the crown through both layers. Cut out the buttonholes, and sew around them using very tightly spaced blanket stitches (see p. 17). If you'd like a stiffer crown, add the interfacing now, and then sew on buttons.

Theodore Giraffe

Wisdom has it that being high above everything is seldom a safe place to be, but the advantage is that from such a position, you can get a unique perspective on things. Imagine being a giraffe for one day . . .

Materials
* child size pink cotton T-shirt with long sleeves
* sharp tapestry needle with large eye

Pattern appears on p. 107

Mouline Thread

		DMC	Anchor
1	1 turquoise	3846	1090
2	1 green	3851	187
3	1 light green	954	203
4	1 red	666	46
5	1 white	Blanc	2

Instructions
Transfer the pattern (see p. 14) to the T-shirt starting at the bottom edge. Follow the pattern and embroider the design using stem stitches (see p. 16) and satin stitches (see p. 19).

Embroider the designs using a sharp tapestry needle with three strands of floss.

Denim Jacket with Embroidered Designs

Most Norwegian national costumes (bunad) are covered with beautiful embroideries. The simple embroidery borders we used to decorate this plain denim jacket are inspired by the handwork done on the costumes in the Telemark region of Norway.

Materials
- adult size denim jacket
- sharp tapestry needle with large eye

Pattern appears on p. 110

Mouline Thread

		DMC	Anchor
1	1 red	666	46
2	1 dark pink	917	88
3	1 light pink	604	55
4	1 dark green	3814	188
5	1 turquoise	3845	1089

Instructions
Trace the patterns (see p. 14) onto the jacket. A simple border is embroidered on the jacket's cuffs and at the bottom edge. Another decoration is embroidered on the collar. Make sure the patterns fit your jacket by adjusting them accordingly. Sew using stem stitches (see p. 16) and satin stitches (see p. 19) as shown on the pattern.

The Princess and the Pea

The romantic fairy tale by Hans Christian Andersen lives in the vivid imagination of children everywhere. The story is brought to life in this sweet piece of handwork for a young child that invites us to play with colors, shapes, and a variety of stitches.

Materials
- child size white T-shirt
- sharp tapestry needle with large eye

Pattern appears on p. 128

Mouline Thread

		DMC	Anchor
1	1 red	666	46
2	1 light pink	605	1094
3	1 pink	603	62
4	1 light purple	3607	87
5	1 orange	970	316
6	1 yellow	444	290
7	1 green	703	238
8	1 turquoise	3846	1090
9	1 light blue	813	161
10	1 purple	3807	122
11	1 plum	718	88

Instructions
Transfer the pattern to the T-shirt (see p. 14). Embroider the designs shown on the pattern using a sharp tapestry needle with three strands of floss. Embroider the outlines for the mattresses and comforters using stem stitches (see p. 16), or similar stitches, before they are filled in with different stitches using the same color of thread.

Embroidered Bed Linens for Baby

Just a few stitches can embellish and enliven bed linens. Traditionally, blue has been used for boys and pink for girls, but there's no reason you can't shake it up a bit (as I did here, with the red floss!) and consider a fresh look that both boys and girls can use.

Materials
* infant-size white cotton comforter cover and pillowcase
* sharp tapestry needle with large eye

Pattern appears on p. 110

Mouline Thread

		DMC	Anchor
■	2 red	666	46

Instructions
Embroider the design using a sharp tapestry needle and three strands of floss. Trace the pattern onto the comforter cover and pillowcase. The two rocking horses with a heart in between are placed in the middle at the top of the comforter cover. Trace one rocking horse onto one side of the pillowcase. Place one heart in each corner of the comforter cover. Embroider the designs shown on the pattern using stem stitches (see p. 16) and satin stitches (see p. 19).

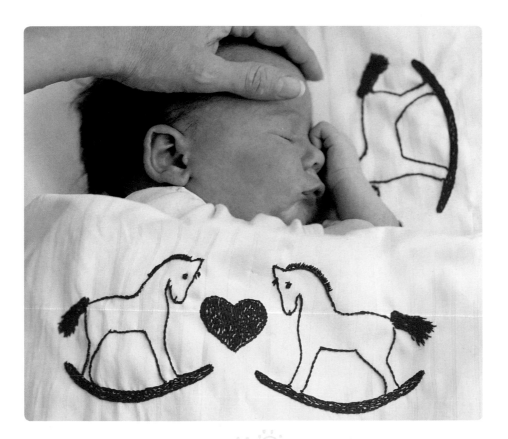

Prima Ballerina Tote Bag

Who didn't dream of becoming a ballerina when they were a child? It's a romantic and beautiful thing to watch a ballet performance — such grace! But it's also very hard work and requires a big commitment on the part of the dancer, so it's only the very best who become prima ballerinas. That doesn't mean you can't have a great ballet bag for all of your necessities.

Materials

- ⚜ 1 piece sturdy linen, such as Rustic weight (7.1 oz) see Resources, p. 95, about 14½" x 36" (37 x 91 cm)
- ⚜ Pink (or another color of your choice) cotton fabric for lining, about 14½" x 36" (37 x 91 cm)
- ⚜ Pink (or another color of your choice) cotton belt webbing, about 1.6 yards (1.5 m) long and 1¼" (3 cm) wide
- ⚜ embroidery hoop (optional)
- ⚜ sewing machine with matching thread

Pattern appears on p. 118

Mouline Thread

		DMC	Anchor
1	1 dark pink	817	13
2	1 light pink 1	603	62
3	1 light pink 2	604	55
4	1 pink 1	151	73
5	1 pink 2	605	1094
6	1 ecru	ecru	892

Instructions

Sew overcast stitches around all the raw edges, then transfer the pattern (see p. 14) onto the fabric. Embroider the outline of the ballerina using a running stitch (see p. 16), and three strands of the lightest color of floss. When you have completed embroidering the figure's outline, finish the outline by "lacing" embroidery floss through every stitch, back and forth, without touching the fabric (see laced running stitch, p. 17). This will give the figure a clear outline. Continue by embroidering the tutu using short and long stitches (see p. 19). For best results, use an embroidery hoop and three strands of floss. Start by using the darkest pink-colored floss at the waist. As you embroider toward the edge of the tutu, the floss should get lighter and lighter pink in color.

The New York skyline is embroidered using one strand of floss. Start by embroidering the outlines of the buildings using backstitches (see p. 16), then fill in the areas inside the outlines by embroidering running stitches (see p. 16) in many different directions.

Embroider "the stage" under the ballerina using backstitches and three strands of floss.

Fold the fabric, right sides facing, and sew the side seams together. Press the seam allowances open. Make a fold at each side at the bottom of the bag, and sew a 2¾" (7 cm)–long seam across at each side. The bag will now have a rectangular bottom. Next, attach the cotton belt webbing to make a strap.

Pin the strap at the sides of the bag with the raw edge facing up toward the top. Attach the strap to the bottom of the bag by sewing at the bottom edge. Fold the strap at the bottom of the bag so it covers the raw edge and conceals it (do this on both sides of the bag). Sew the strap to the bag on both sides, a little below the location of the raw edge. Then sew the strap to the bag at the top on both sides.

Follow the instructions above to sew the lining to the bag. Press all seam allowances open, and pull the lining over the bag, right sides facing. Sew along the top of the bag, about ⅜" (1 cm) from the edge, and leave about a 4" (10 cm)–long opening so that you can turn the bag right side out. Sew the opening closed, and lightly press the top seam.

Resources

EMBROIDERY FLOSS

DMC

- *Purl Soho*
  459 Broome St.
  New York, NY 10013
  (212) 420-8796
  www.purlsoho.com

- *Annie & Company Needlepoint and Knitting*
  1763 2nd Ave. Corner of 92nd St.
  New York, NY 10128
  SW Corner of 92nd St. & 2nd Ave.
  For needlepoint and knitting inquiries,
  (212) 360-7266
  For needlepoint inquiries,
    E-mail annie@annieandco.com
  For knitting inquiries,
    E-mail anniesknitting@gmail.com
  www.annieandco.com

- *Jo-Ann Stores*
  www.joann.com

Anchor Floss

- *Yarn Tree*
  An online wholesaler that which lists all the stores
  they service with Anchor Floss (and others).
  www.yarntree.com

YARN

Dale Baby Wool

- *Dale Yarn North America*
  www.dalegarnnorthamerica.com

- *Wooly Baa Baa*
  www.woolybaabaa.com

- *Halycon Yarn*
  Carries a partial selection.
  www.halyconyarn.com

- *Mango Moon Yarns*
  E-mail: info@mangomoonyarns.com

Prism Yarns

www.prismyarn.com
(for store locations only)

Rauma Baby Panda

- *Nordic Fiber Arts*
  www.nordicfiberarts.com
  E-mail: nordicfiberarts@yahoo.com

MARKERS

Collins Vanishing Fabric Marker (purple)

A safe way of marking for the short-time project,
marks start to disappear within 12 to 24 hours

- *Jo-Ann Stores*
  www.joann.com

- *Amazon*
  www.amazon.com

Vanishing Fabric Marker

A bright purple mark that does not vanish within
48 hours. Marks may be removed by washing in
cold water.

- *Sewing Parts Online*
  www.sewingpartsonline.com

Washable Wonder Marker (blue)

Makes a bright blue mark on fabric
that can easily be removed with plain water.
Works great on lighter-color acrylic fabrics; not
recommended for use on dark fabrics.

- *Sail Rite*
  www.sailrite.com

Bohin Ultra Fine Blue Washable Wonder Marker

Makes a bright blue mark, and features an extra-
fine point for thin lines. Marks are easily removed
with plain water.

- *Amazon*
  www.amazon.com

Bohin Extra-Fine Chalk Pencil

A water-soluble marker with an extra-fine lead. It can be washed out or erased with any fabric eraser.

- *Amazon*
  www.amazon.com

Clover White Marking Fine Pen

Great for dark fabric, ink doesn't show until dry. Marks can be removed with a steam iron or water.

- *Amazon*
  www.amazon.com

CORSETS & BUSTIERS

- *Milanoo*
  www.milanoo.com

- *Light in the Box*
  www.lightinthebox.com

ACCESSORIES FOR SUSPENDERS

- *Suspender Store*
  www.suspenderstore.com
  E-mail: info@suspenderstore.com

- *A Tailored Suit*
  www.atailoredsuit.com

- *Articles of Style*
  www.articlesofstyle.com

BIKINI CLASPS

- *Amazon*
  www.amazon.com

NEEDLEPOINT CANVAS

- *Amazon*
  www.amazon.com

- *Needlepoint US*
  www.needlepointus.com

- *Jo-Ann Stores*
  www.joann.com

WATCHBAND BUCKLES AND CLASPS

- *Watchband Center*
  They carry a wide selection of buckles and clasps for watches. Ships worldwide
  www.watch-band-center.com

- *Esslinger*
  Esslinger is a leading Internet provider of watchmaker's supplies. Ships from the U.S.
  www.esslinger.com

LINEN

- *Fabric Store*
  Carries 100% "Rustic" Linen, heavy weight (7.1 oz/yd2) This 100% linen is referred to as "Rustic" due to its more textured look and feel. Durable and perfect for projects that require just a bit more substance. Available in several colors including bleached white. Ships from the U.S.
  www.fabrics-store.com

PURSE CLASPS

- *Amazon*
  www.amazon.com

- *Jo-Ann Stores*
  www.joann.com

Patterns

All patterns are 100% unless otherwise noted. Some patterns will need to be enlarged on a photocopier.

Party Corset with Stylized Roses, p. 70
100% of actual size

Party Corset with Stylized Roses, p. 70
100% of actual size

Made with Love, p. 24
100% of actual size

Made with Love, p. 24
100% of actual size

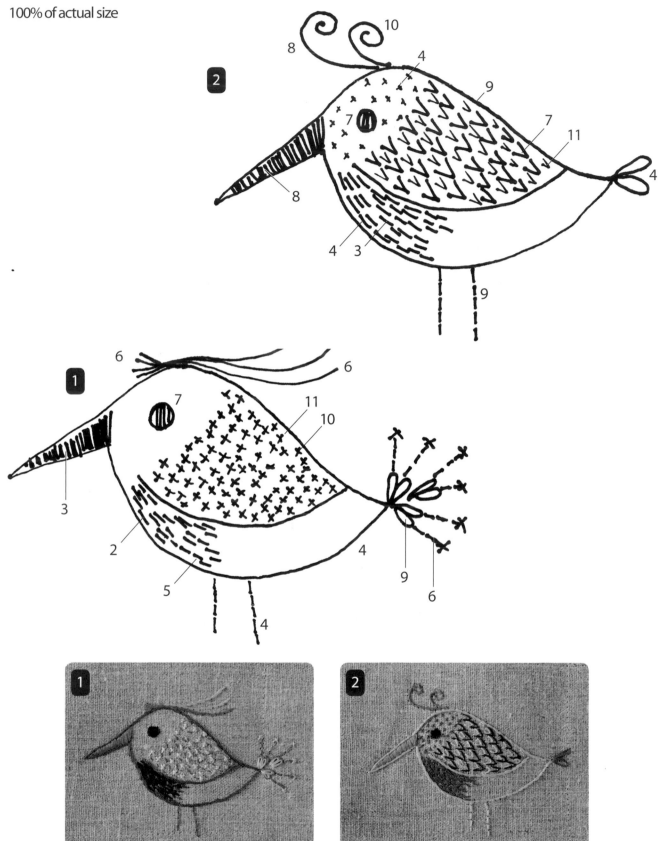

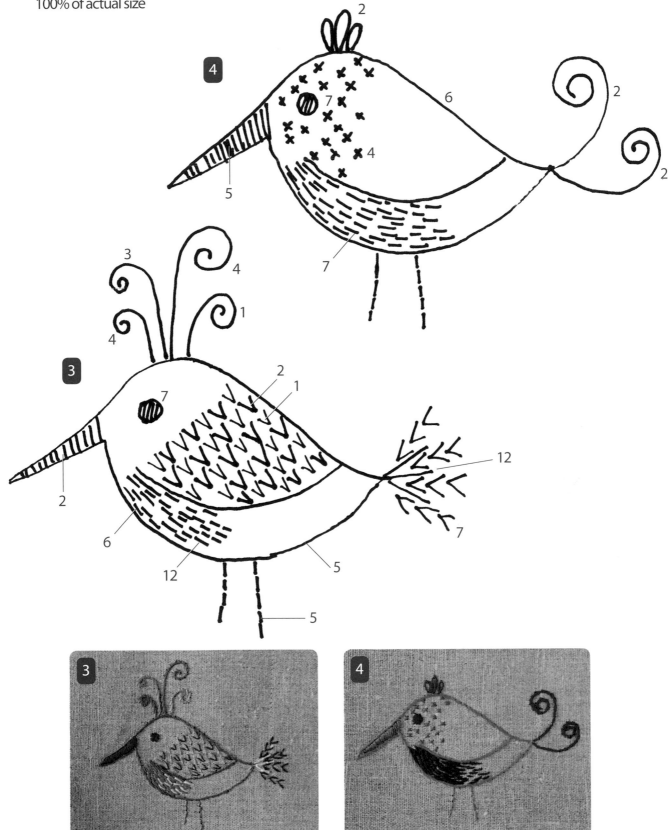

For the Math Lover, p. 52
100% of actual size

$$\frac{7 \cdot 6}{42}$$

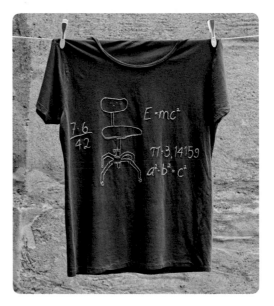

For the Math Lover, p. 52
100% of actual size

$$E = mc^2$$

$$\pi = 3,14159$$

$$a^2 + b^2 = c^2$$

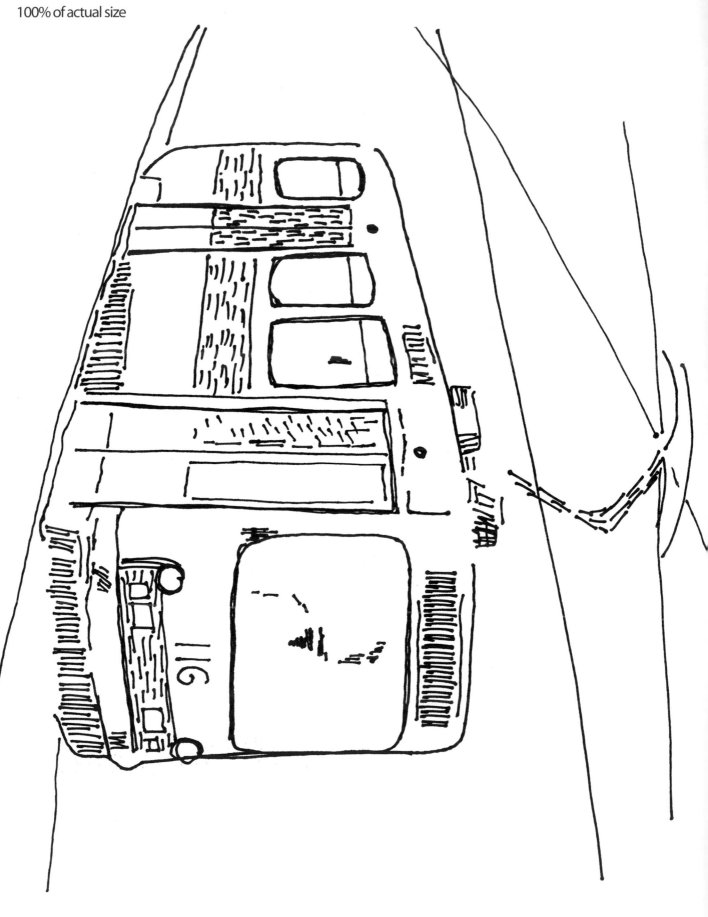

4

1

1

5

1

2

3

1

2

3

1

2

1

3

2

2

1

2

3

1

1

2

3

1

2

1

3

1

Princess Dress with Wild Strawberries, p. 64
100% of actual size

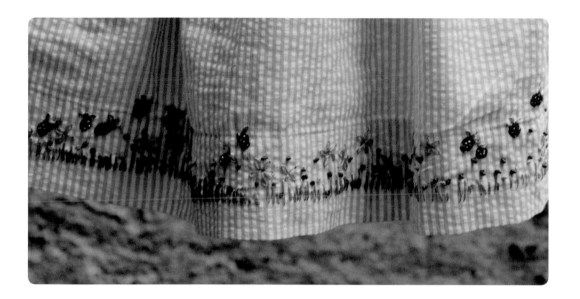

Princess Dress with Wild Strawberries, p. 64
100% of actual size

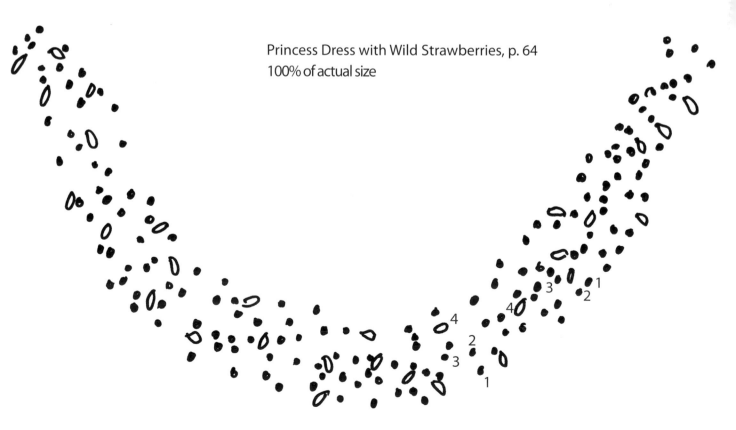

Denim Jacket with
Embroidered Designs, p. 86
100% of actual size

Embroidered Bed Linens for Baby, p. 90
100% of actual size

110

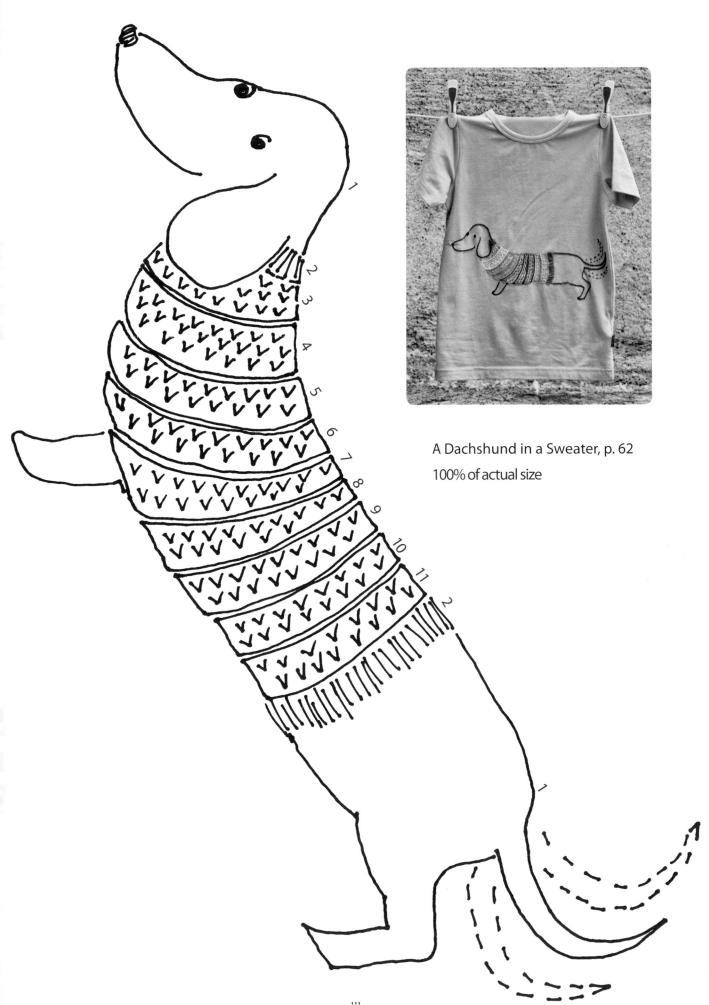

A Dachshund in a Sweater, p. 62

100% of actual size

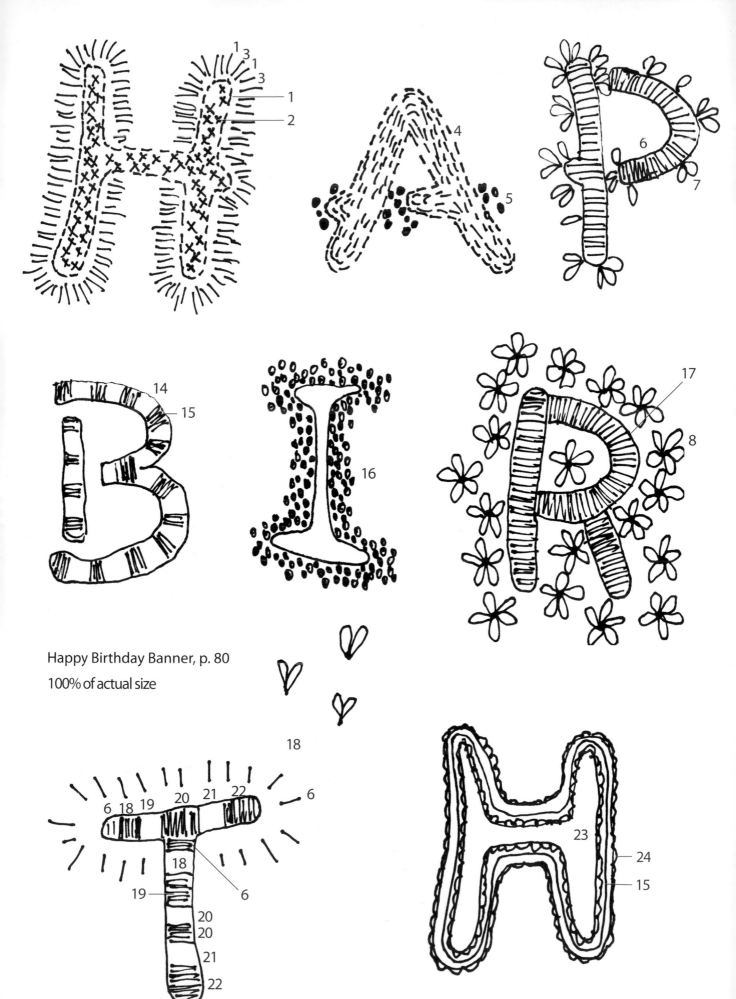

Happy Birthday Banner, p. 80

100% of actual size

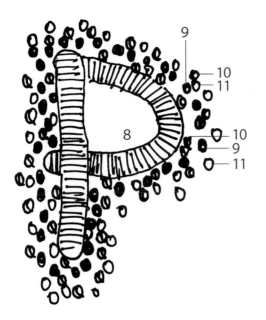

9
10
11
8
10
9
11

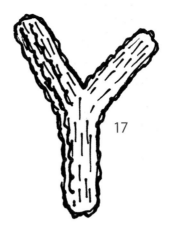

17

25

23

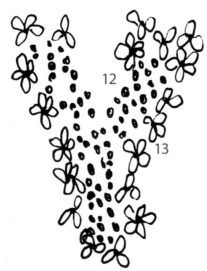

12
13

Happy Birthday Banner, p. 80

100% of actual size

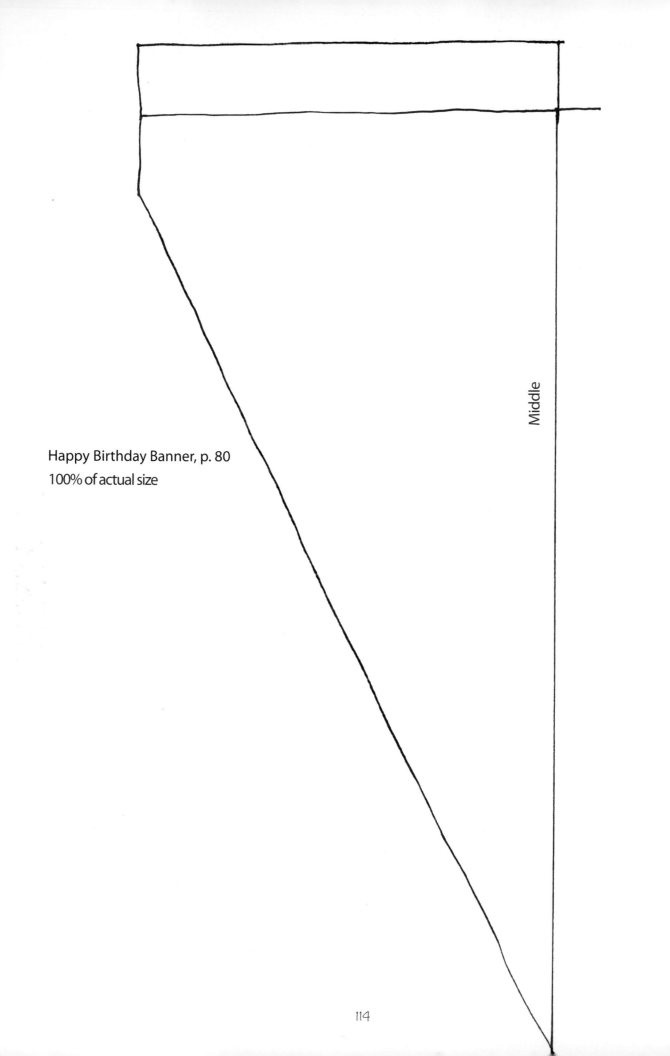

Happy Birthday Banner, p. 80
100% of actual size

Middle

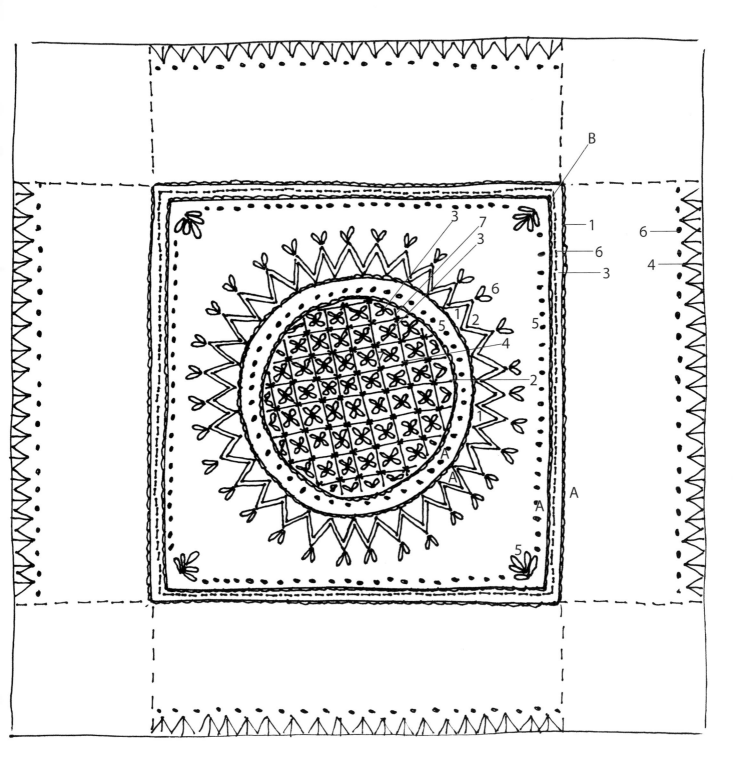

Beetles and Dragonflies, p. 44
100% of actual size

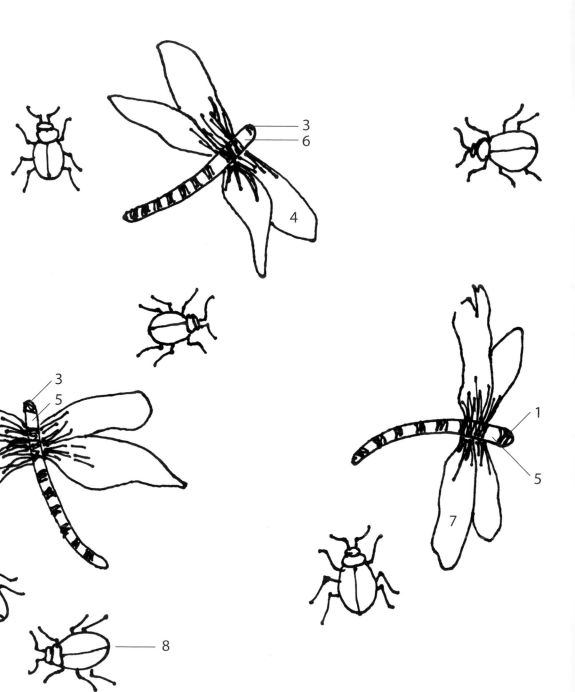

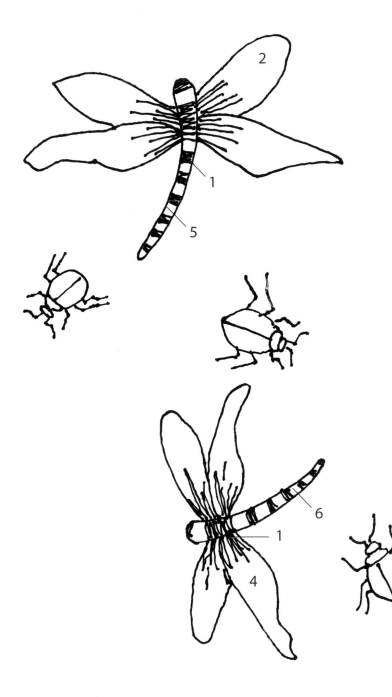

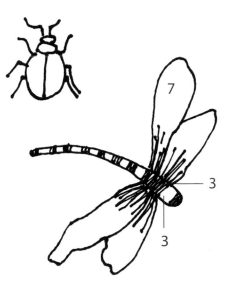

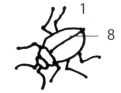

Prima Ballerina Canvas Bag, p. 92
65% of actual size;
enlarge by 135%

1

2

70% of actual size;
enlarge by 130%

Crocodile Loves Cupcakes, p. 72

4

5

6

3

100% of actual size

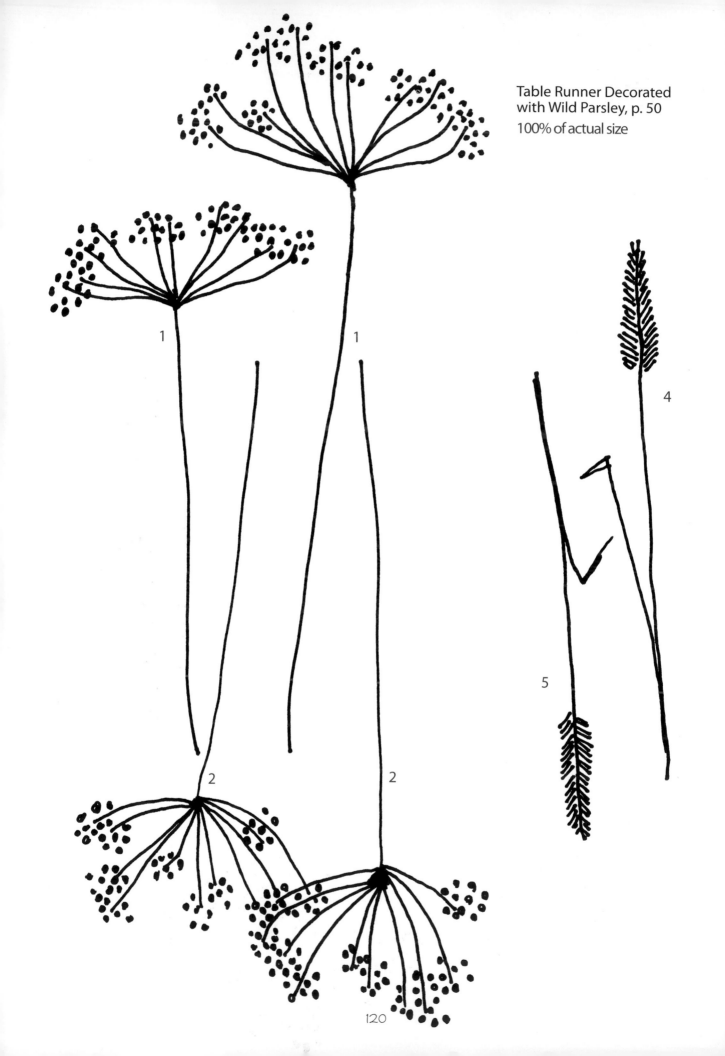

Table Runner Decorated
with Wild Parsley, p. 50
100% of actual size

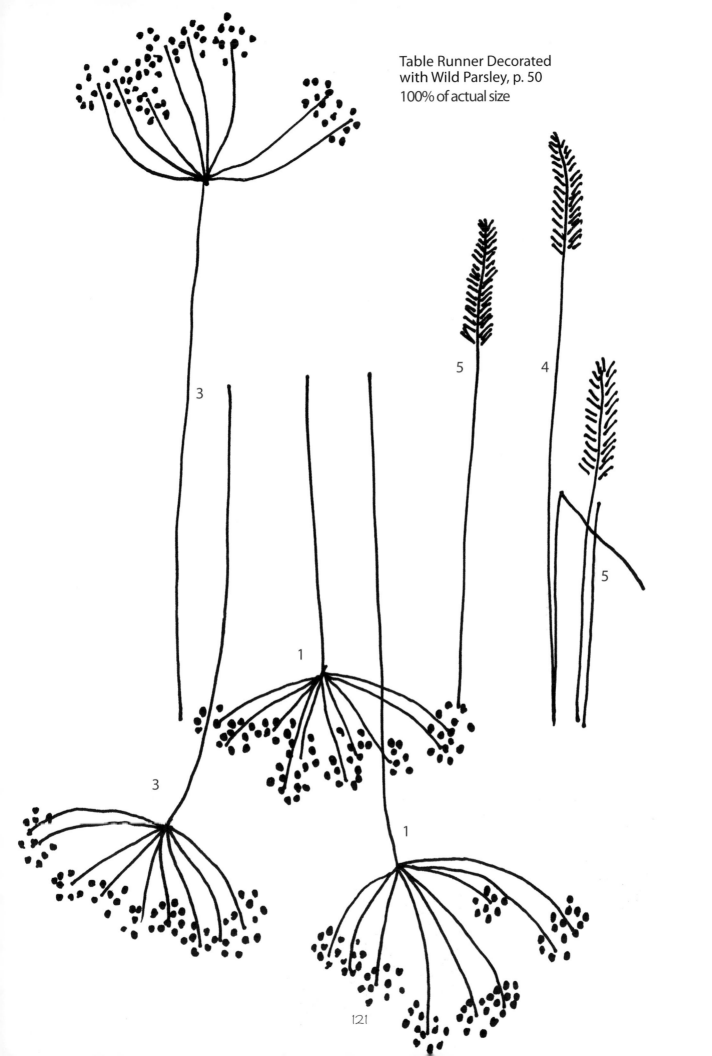

Table Runner Decorated
with Wild Parsley, p. 50
100% of actual size

Table Runner Decorated
with Wild Parsley, p. 50

100% of actual size

3

3

5

5

Table Runner Decorated
with Wild Parsley, p. 50
100% of actual size

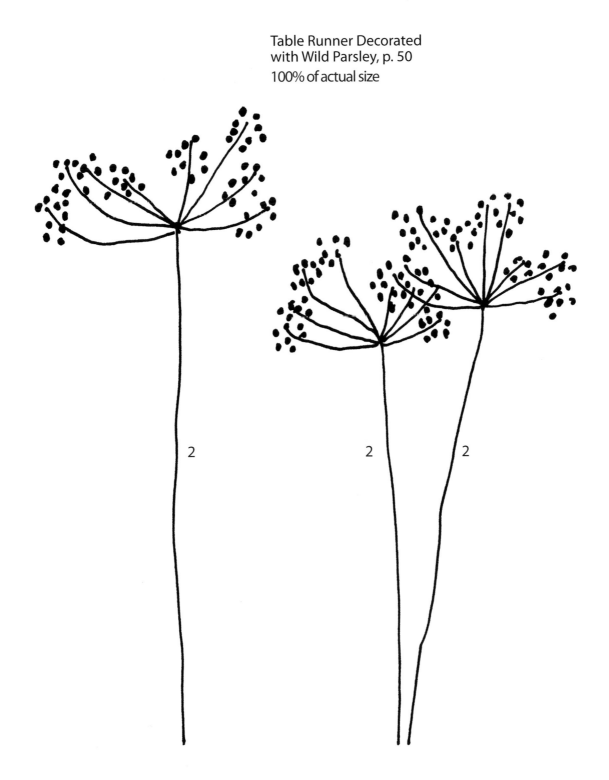

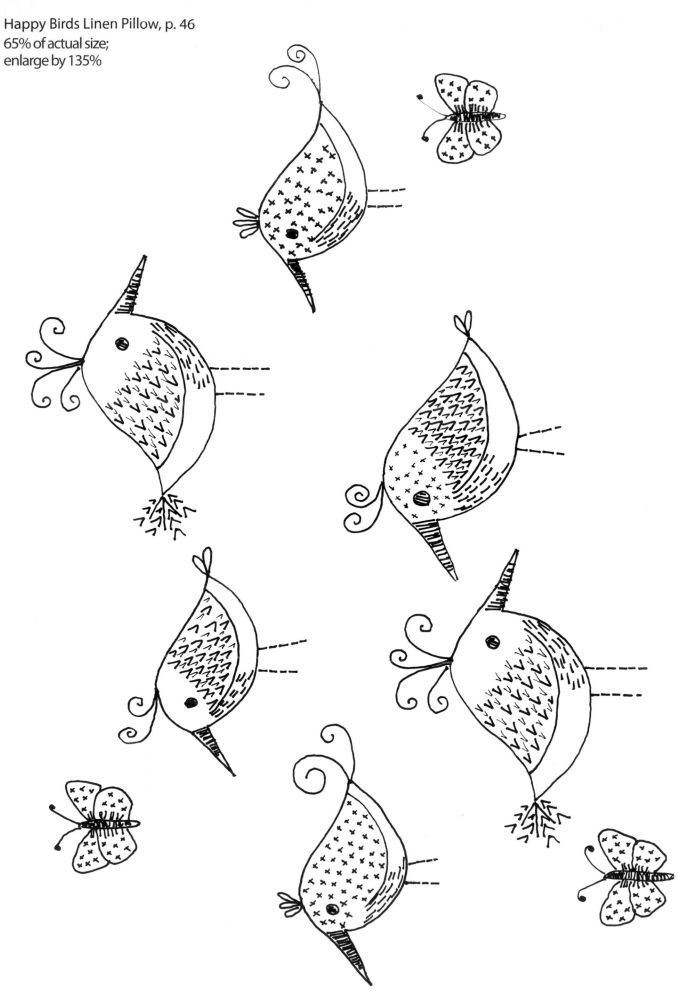

Happy Birthday Crown, p. 82

80% of actual size;
enlarge by 120%

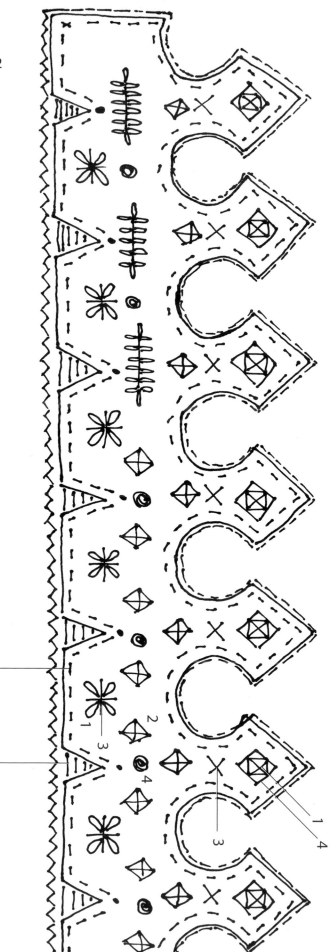